GEORG BÜCHNER

WORLD DRAMATISTS / *General Editor: Lina Mainiero*
In the same series:

Edward Albee	*Ronald Hayman*
Jean Anouilh	*Lewis W. Falb*
Samuel Beckett	*Ronald Hayman*
Bertolt Brecht	*Karl H. Schoeps*
Georg Büchner	*William C. Reeve*
Pedro Calderón de la Barca	*Heinz Gerstinger*
Anton Chekhov	*Siegfried Melchinger*
Euripides	*Siegfried Melchinger*
Georges Feydeau	*Leonard C. Pronko*
Carlo Goldoni	*Heinz Riedt*
Oliver Goldsmith and	
Richard Brinsley Sheridan	*Marlies K. Danziger*
Henrik Ibsen	*Hans Georg Meyer*
Eugène Ionesco	*Ronald Hayman*
Christopher Marlowe	*Gerald Pinciss*
Arthur Miller	*Ronald Hayman*
Molière	*Gertrud Mander*
Sean O'Casey	*Doris daRin*
John Osborne	*Ronald Hayman*
Harold Pinter	*Ronald Hayman*
Luigi Pirandello	*Renate Matthaei*
Friedrich Schiller	*Charles E. Passage*
Arthur Schnitzler	*Reinhard Urbach*
Shakespeare's Histories	*George J. Becker*
Shakespeare's Tragedies	*Phyllis Rackin*
Bernard Shaw	*Pat M. Carr*
Sophocles	*Siegfried Melchinger*
August Strindberg	*Gunnar Ollén*
Lope de Vega and	
Spanish Drama	*Heinz Gerstinger*
Arnold Wesker	*Ronald Hayman*

GEORG

ÜCHNER

WILLIAM C. REEVE

WITH PHOTOGRAPHS

FREDERICK UNGAR PUBLISHING CO.
NEW YORK

Copyright © 1979 by Frederick Ungar
   Publishing Co., Inc.
Printed in the United States of America
Designed by Edith Fowler

Library of Congress Cataloging in Publication Data
Reeve, William C   1943–
   Georg Büchner.
   (World dramatists)
   Bibliography: p
   Includes index
   1. Büchner, George, 1813–1837—Criticism and in-
terpretation
PT1828.B6R38   832'.7   77-4599
ISBN 0-8044-2711-9

CONTENTS

	Chronology	I
1.	The Life and Times of Georg Büchner	5
2.	Büchner's View of Art: *Lenz*	25
3.	*Danton's Death*	47
4.	*Leonce and Lena*	87
5.	*Woyzeck*	122
6.	Conclusion: The Büchner Phenomenon	161
	Notes	166
	Bibliography	173
	Index	179

CHRONOLOGY

1813   Georg Büchner is born on 17 October in the small town of Goddelau near Darmstadt, Germany, the first child of Dr. Ernst Büchner.

1816   The Büchner family moves to Darmstadt where Georg goes to a private school.

1825   Georg attends the Darmstadt high school (Gymnasium).

1831   He enrolls in medicine at the University of Strasbourg on 9 November and begins to frequent the meetings of the students' association "Eugenia," while living at the home of Pastor Johann Jakob Jaegle.

1833   In July he journeys through the Vosges mountains.
       Becomes secretly engaged to his host's daughter, Minna Jaegle.
       Enrolls as a student of medicine at the University of Giessen, as required by local law. In November falls sick with meningitis and is forced to return to Darmstadt in December to convalesce. Begins a serious study of the French Revolution.

1834   He comes back to Giessen in January and meets Pastor Friedrich Ludwig Weidig, a member of a liberal revolutionary group.
       Founds "The Society for the Rights of Man"

after the French model in Giessen, and later another branch in Darmstadt.

Starts to write a political pamphlet, *The Hessian Messenger*.

Travels to Strasbourg to see his fiancée. Their engagement is finally announced.

First edition of *The Hessian Messenger* as revised by Pastor Weidig is printed on 31 July. On the same day, the conspiracy is betrayed to the authorities by one of its members, J. K. Kuhl. One of the conspirators is arrested and Büchner sets out to warn friends.

Several members of "The Society for the Rights of Man" are arrested in September. Büchner manages to conceal his complicity.

1835   Further arrests and Büchner is asked to appear before the investigating authorities.

From about the middle of January to the end of February, he writes *Danton's Death* to finance his escape.

On 1 March he leaves for the French border to avoid arrest, eventually crossing on 9 March.

A partial publication of *Danton's Death* in a periodical.

A warrant is issued for the arrest of Georg Büchner on 13 June in Darmstadt.

In July *Danton's Death* is issued in its entirety but with unauthorized changes, the only work to appear in print during Büchner's lifetime.

Translates Victor Hugo's plays *Lucretia Borgia* and *Maria Tudor*.

Begins his study of the German dramatist Jakob Michael Lenz, the result of which is the short story *Lenz*.

Works on his university thesis concerning the nervous system of a fish ("Mémoire sur le système nerveux du barbeau").

1836   Reads his thesis at three meetings of the Society of Natural Science in Strasbourg.

Writes his only comedy, *Leonce and Lena*

(April-June), inspired by a competition spon-
sored by the Cotta Publishing House.
Begins to work on *Woyzeck*.
Receives his doctor's degree from the Univer-
sity of Zurich and the offer of a faculty position.
Moves to Zurich on 18 October.
Gives an inaugural lecture on cranial nerves.
Continues work on *Woyzeck*.
Commences to offer a lecture course in compara-
tive anatomy.

1837 2 February, first signs of his fatal illness, typhus.
Büchner dies 19 February.

1838 *Leonce and Lena* published in incomplete form
by Karl Gutzkow.

1839 *Lenz* appears in print, again through the efforts
of Gutzkow.

1850 Büchner's brother, Ludwig, brings out an edition of Büchner's works, excluding *Woyzeck*.

1879 First complete works edited by Karl Emil
Franzos.

1885 Première of *Leonce and Lena*, 31 May, in
Munich.

1902 First performance of *Danton's Death*, 5 January,
in Berlin.

1913 An important public performance of *Danton's
Death* and première of *Woyzeck*, 8 November,
in Munich.

1916 Max Reinhardt's first staging of *Danton's
Death*, 15 December, in Berlin.

1922 Appearance of Fritz Bergemann's complete edition.

1925 Alban Berg's opera *Wozzeck* is premièred, 14
December in Berlin.

1967 Publication of the first volume of Werner R.
Lehmann's critical edition *Georg Büchner: Complete Works and Letters*, which includes the
four drafts of *Woyzeck*.

1. THE LIFE AND TIMES OF GEORG BÜCHNER

Despite the fact that Büchner has been rightly called a precursor of several literary movements, ranging from naturalism through expressionism to the theater of the absurd, he was nonetheless a phenomenon in a specific historic setting. To appreciate fully his achievement, one must have some understanding of the period of European history referred to as the Restoration where anachronism and reaction became a political way of life. Royal heads of government, under political and economic duress during the wars of liberation against Napoleon's continental system, agreed to grant constitutions and democratic reforms according to the principles that had grown out of the French Revolution. However, by the year 1815 and the time of the Congress of Vienna, Prince Metternich—the embodiment of Restoration politics—and the German princes conveniently forgot their promises of providing constitutional government and attempted to placate the people with a few democratic but ineffectual sops. The majority of the population, farmers, peasants, only recently released from medieval systems of near serfdom, or the industrial class, which was just beginning to appear as an economic force on the continent, blindly accepted conditions little differing from those prior to the wars of liberation. An old tradition of unquestioned obedience was long to be abused and exploited by the ruling powers.

After the fall of Napoleon, Ludwig I, the Grand Duke of Hesse, attempted to turn back the clock with the reestablishment of an eighteenth-century autocratic regime. Although a conservative constitution was granted in 1820, the head of state preserved his traditional powers; some of the local aristocrats still had the right to demand the performance of certain feudal duties from the peasants, and oppressive taxes and social conditions rendered life difficult for the lower classes. Bad harvests also contributed to the state of poverty to which many of the peasants were reduced and which led to the emigration of thousands to America. When in 1830 Ludwig II, as a condition of his accession, demanded that Hesse pay his private debts of some two million gulden, the peasants expressed their disapproval by an uprising, which was repressed by the Grand Duke's minister du Thil. Although the political struggle continued, by 1832 most of the democratic measures guaranteed by the 1820 constitution had been annulled. However, the foundations of the Restoration were not fated to rest completely unassailed. A number of idealistically motivated young men, largely from intellectual centers such as universities and the Church, began to demand fulfillment of the constitutional promises by petition and even open rebellion. This group, primarily from the well-to-do sections of the middle class, suffered persecution from the authorities, and many ended their lives either in jail or in exile.

Georg Büchner was born on 17 October 1813 in the small town of Goddelau, Hesse, the oldest of six children. His father, Ernst Karl, had served as a doctor with the Dutch troops in Napoleon's army. Fond of French culture and eighteenth-century rationalist philosophy, he often read aloud to his family newspaper excerpts that dealt with the history of the French Revolution.

Unlike her free-thinking physician husband, Frau Büchner was a devout Christian. She had a cheerful disposition and was especially fond of literature, particularly the works of Friedrich Schiller. From all accounts it was a happy marriage. When, in 1816, Ernst Büchner was promoted to a medical position in Darmstadt, the whole family moved to the ducal city and young Georg was enrolled in a private school. From 1825 until the spring of 1831 he attended the Ludwig Georgs Gymnasium, the local high school. Reports of fellow students and his school essays give evidence of a marked enthusiasm for literature, especially Shakespeare, Goethe, and the early Greek writers, a glorification of freedom and human reason, and a strong sense of social responsibility towards the less fortunate. For example, Büchner calls the struggles for religious freedom on the part of four hundred citizens of Pforzheim during the Thirty Years' War "the first act of the great struggle that humanity wages against its oppressors just as the French Revolution was the second."[1]

In the autumn of 1831 at the instigation of his father, Büchner began to attend the University of Strasbourg, where he studied philosophy and the natural sciences, including zoology and comparative anatomy. The decision to register at a French university had been dictated by the high quality of the Strasbourg medical school, the atmosphere of French culture in what was once a German city, and the presence of a distant relative, the theologian Eduard Reuss. Büchner found living quarters in the home of the Lutheran pastor Jaegle, to whose daughter Louise Wilhelmine, Minna for short, he later became secretly engaged. Strasbourg represented the turning point in Büchner's life. It was here that he came in contact with one of the most liberal centers in Europe, Strasbourg harbored a large percentage of those German political refugees who were forced to flee across the border. We know more about this intellectually productive period in Büchner's life than about any other because of the survival of some sixty letters, which, miraculously, neither his fiancée nor a fire in the Büchner home in Darmstadt managed to destroy. He attended meetings of a local students' club, Eugenia, where he is reported to have denounced the corruption of the autocratic German governments, and he became involved with the activities of the local branch of a revolutionary group called The Society for the Rights of Man and Citizen.

Büchner's earliest Strasbourg letters to his parents, such as that of 4 December 1831, offer a description of student participation in liberal agitation. But one is immediately aware of his attitude to these street spectacles—that of aloof distance. Regarding the scene from the vantage point of an observer, not an active participant, he depicts the triumphant entry of a Polish-Italian rebel leader with wit and occasional satire, reducing it to the level of theater: "and the performance is over."

The St. Simonist movement—which advocated

greater sexual freedom, the emancipation of women, a new morality based on both nature and reason, and a socially just community achieved by a redistribution of property—also undergoes Büchner's skeptical appraisal. A letter depicts one of his university acquaintances, Rousseau, a St. Simonist, who had tried unsuccessfully to enter Germany to preach to the people. Although as an individual Rousseau rates highly in the affections of the author, as a St. Simonist he becomes the unwitting victim of a few satiric barbs, as Büchner resolves that he "would like to become a St. Simonist out of sheer laziness, for people would have to honor fittingly [his] capacity in this regard." This incident is mentioned here as an indication of Büchner's critical awareness of a branch of the liberal movement noted for its social-revolutionary tendencies.

On 3 April 1833, a group of fifty conspirators, including several students, tried unsuccessfully to storm a military guardhouse in Frankfurt. By this exemplary and symbolic act, they had hoped to spread the flame of revolutionary enthusiasm over the whole of Germany. This Frankfurt Putsch was easily put down with little loss of life, but many arrests were made and measures of repression, such as increased censorship and the disbanding of fraternities, were put into effect. It was during the aftermath of this fiasco that Büchner, in accordance with a regulation which obliged each citizen of Hesse to spend a minimum of four semesters at the State University of Giessen, returned to Germany and examined the failure of the uprising. A note of increased disillusionment with the aims of the Liberals begins to creep into his correspondence. From Darmstadt he wrote to a friend on 9 December

1833: "The political situation could drive me mad. The poor people patiently drag the cart upon which the princes and the Liberals perform their monkey's comedy. Each evening I pray for hemp and lanterns." All liberal agitation is impatiently rejected as a "monkey's comedy," while the writer finds solace only in "hemp and lanterns," the symbols of the violence necessary for the success of the French Revolution. Büchner possesses the perspicacity to see that the Liberals, denied an active role in the political affairs of Europe, found comfort in ineffectual meetings, humanistically motivated but pragmatically unrealizable projects, and their literary output. Disdaining to resort to literature as an escape and refusing to avail himself of the expediency of the Romantics who "always reach back to the Middle Ages because they cannot fill a place in the present," he gave early evidence of the direction his literary and political career would take.

Whereas we sense that Büchner had some sympathy for the bourgeoisie, coming from that class himself, as far as his opinion of the aristocracy is concerned, there can be no doubt that it is characterized by scorn and hatred. "God may be merciful to their most illustrious, annointed blockheads; hopefully on earth they won't find any more mercy." The grounds for his animosity are explained to his family in a letter from Giessen dated February 1834, in which he justifies hate as an active force, equally effective as love, to right social injustice. No man, regardless of his noble birth or the advantages he enjoys through education, has the right to scorn his fellow man. "The aristocratic concept is the most disgraceful form of contempt for the Holy Spirit in man; against it I turn its own weapons: arrogance against arrogance, mockery against mockery." The sanctity of the individual demands that every man, even the lowest, have our love and respect. It will become more and more evident in our examination of Büchner that he was a man who felt more than he thought, was emotional rather than logical. His letters and his final work *Woyzeck* bear evidence of a sincere, heart-felt affection for "a healthy, strong people." He stated his preference for the company of his boot-polisher rather than that of an educated gentleman, and detesting the pretentious vocal exercises of the concert or *soirée*, he found true musical pleasure in native folk songs, which he incorporated so effectively into his own literary works.

Büchner's interest in the lower class was motivated primarily by his deep concern for human suffering. What segment of the population sustained more injustice than the Hessian peasants who in certain areas were still legally considered serfs? Büchner quite naturally turned to the question of how to improve the material lot of the oppressed and came up with an answer closely approximating the conclusion reached by Karl Marx. "I will of course always act according to my principles, but recently I have learned that only the necessary needs of the great mass can bring about changes, that all the activity and screaming of individuals is the work of fools done in vain." For Büchner the hero of progress could no longer be the heroic individual, but rather the group or class. Individualism must be submerged and consumed in one single social will which will serve the community as a whole. Fully convinced of the ineffectiveness of independent action, he determined to refrain from engaging in "the local politics and childish revolutionary pranks of Giessen."

Just how did Büchner perceive that the people would achieve the desired new order? "If in our age something is to help, then it's violence." This advocation of force and the subsequent destruction of the status quo were justified in the eyes of the young student both by the "state of violence" already existing in Germany and by the apparent impossibility of realizing any effective transformation by peaceful means. The German people must rise and forcibly win back the rights with which each man is born.

In pointing to the manner in which the masses would be incited to revolt, we note a radical innovation in the history of German thought. The early nineteenth century witnessed the rise into prominence of the philosophical movement of German idealism, systems representing some of the greatest monuments of pure conceptual thought. Since Büchner was faced with the depressing view of human degradation caused by material circumstances, he abnegated this idealistic tradition as illusion and insisted upon the pragmatic necessity of coming to terms with reality. "The relationship between poor and rich is the only revolutionary element in the world; hunger alone can become the goddess of freedom, and only a Moses who sent down upon us the seven plagues of Egypt could be a Messiah. Fatten the peasants and the revolution suffers from apoplexy." It is not the visions of idealistically motivated individuals that produce revolutions but rather crass economic motives. The demagogue who speaks to the masses about human rights, the equality of man, or universal brotherhood is only wasting his time. To appeal to the peasant's empty stomach, however, to point out his empty wallet, this alone will make an impression upon his mind and incite him to some positive action on his own behalf.

This note of political activism stands in marked contrast with the general mood of dissatisfaction and depression characterizing the year Büchner spent in Giessen. At one point, he was forced to return to the family home in Darmstadt to recover from a serious attack of meningitis, and it was from here that, having begun a detailed examination of the French Revolution, he wrote the famous letter to his fiancée, outlining his sense of helplessness, despair, and frustration vis-à-vis an irrational historic force.

> I was studying the history of the [French] Revolution. I felt as if I were utterly destroyed by the horrible fatalism of history. I find in human nature a terrible uniformity, in human relations an unavoidable force granted to all and to no one. The individual is only foam upon the wave, greatness a case of mere chance, the rule of the genius a puppet play, a ridiculous struggle against an iron law. To recognize this law is man's greatest achievement, to control it impossible. . . . I am becoming accustomed to the sight of blood. But I'm no guillotine blade. "Must" is one of the words of damnation with which man has been baptized. The saying: "for it must needs be that offences come, but woe to that man by whom the offence cometh!" [Matthew 18:7]—is horrible! What is it that lies, murders, steals in us? I don't like to pursue this thought.

An apparent contradiction now appears in the life of Büchner. Despite the above insight, which would reject any individual attempt to effect political change as foolish, Büchner, on his return to Giessen, founded The Society for the Rights of Man after the French model and became actively involved with a liberal revolutionary group under the leadership of Pastor

Friedrich Ludwig Weidig. The result of this coalition was the writing of *The Hessian Messenger*, a pamphlet intended to incite the Hessian peasants to engage in open revolt.

"If ever the Revolution is to be executed in a decisive manner, this can and may only occur through the great mass of the people by whose superiority in number and weight the soldiers would have to be, as it were, crushed. It is therefore a question of winning this great mass and this at present can only happen through pamphlets."[2] At the time when Büchner wrote *The Hessian Messenger*, he assumed, as Marx later put it, the role of the intellectual as one who comprehends the historical process and, motivated by youthful idealism, joins the battle of the class conflict on the side of the people. His view of life, we may assume, remained essentially humanistic, for, as in the case of all revolutionists, he must have had faith in man's essential goodness, a virtue to be developed and perfected by rationally oriented revisions of society.

In any analysis of Büchner's first work, one is hampered by the problem that the political pamphlet that has come down to us does not represent the original draft as Büchner proposed to have it printed. The essay is the result of the forced collaboration between a pastor and an active adherent of the liberal movement—Friedrich Ludwig Weidig—and a young revolutionist with marked communist inclinations— Georg Büchner. From the investigations conducted by the authorities after the failure of the conspiracy and from statements made by associates, it is clear that Büchner formulated the initial draft, but that it was much too extreme in the eyes of Pastor Weidig, who still hoped to gain the support of an enlightened bourgeoisie in the establishment of a democracy. Having had the first version presented for his approval, he proceeded to make several alterations and additions, toning down the radical, more revolutionary sentiment of the original. For example, Büchner's "the rich" is replaced by "the aristocrats." By this substitution, Weidig obviously intended to attack only the nobility, while sparing the middle class which, of course, would have been included in Büchner's more comprehensive and basic designation "the rich." All of Weidig's additions, as might be expected from a minister of the Lutheran Church, amount to a religious justification of the Hessian uprising, supported by numerous quotations and parallels drawn from the Bible. Nonetheless, the pamphlet, as it was finally printed and distributed, still represents essentially the spirit of one man, Georg Büchner.

Stylistically Büchner composed *The Hessian Messenger* on the basis of contrast. From the opening epigraph to the concluding words, he continually points out the disparity between the haves and the have-nots, reinforced by biblical imagery and the language of agronomics, two sources familiar to the Hessian peasants, and thus calculated to make a strong emotional appeal. Extensive use is also made of rhetorical questions intentionally designed to point out the glaring absurdity and injustice of the situation.

Structurally, the pamphlet may be divided into three major sections. The first and most extensive contains a list of social and economic grievances directed against the Grand Duchy of Hesse with an appeal to the people to throw off the shackles of exploitation and subjugation. After a brief description of the ideal society with a democratic form of government, *The*

Hessian Messenger concludes with an outline of the reactionary movement in Europe.

The motto—"Peace to the huts! War on the palaces!"—borrowed from the French Revolution, sets up the basic dichotomy: peasant versus aristocrat, poverty versus wealth. In this succinct expression of ultimate aims, we detect Rousseauesque overtones: the goodness, tranquility, and simplicity of rural life set in contrast with the luxury, intrigue, and corruption of the more sophisticated but artificial urban life. The choice of "war" openly proclaims the rejection of peaceful means in favor of violent upheaval, a declaration of war on the forces of human injustice.

The essay proper commences with one of Weidig's additions, in which he transmuted a simple uprising into a type of holy war ordained by God. In 1836, from exile in France, Büchner wrote to Karl Gutzkow: "There are only two levers capable of moving the great class [i.e. the people]: material wretchedness and religious fanaticism." It is evident that Büchner recognized religion as a useful tool, capable of inciting the pious peasants to revolt. In this sense, Büchner could easily have justified the use of divine sanction without fear of contradicting his more pragmatic approach.

The part first attributed to Büchner establishes the essential dichotomy that will be repeated on numerous occasions and under various guises until the end of the essay. On the one hand we have the idle, overfed rich, wallowing in excess, while on the other hand, we are encouraged to sympathize with the overworked, poverty-stricken peasants, who are mere dung on the fields as far as the "haves" are concerned. The aristocracy, which treats the farmer no better than an ox or a slave, exploits the masses who do not enjoy the fruits of their labor. "[The rich man] takes the grain and leaves [the peasant] the stubble. . . . His sweat is the salt on the rich man's table."

Economics becomes the major issue as Büchner reviewed the governing structure of the Grand Duchy. The financial income exacted from the people to support this body he derogatorily labels "the blood tithe." This exploitation is carried on in the name of the state, a political system supported by restoration politics and created to preserve the special position of the rulers at the expense of the people. The oppressors justify their actions by reference to the government, which in turn maintains that its measures are necessary to preserve "order"—the status quo. Büchner, however, asked What constitutes the state? "If a number of people live in a country and there are ordinances and laws in existence according to which each must conduct himself, then it is said they form a state. The state is therefore *all people*; the regulators in the state are the laws by which the welfare of *all people* is assured and which are to be derived from the welfare of *all people*." These ideals were in all likelihood derived from the famous "Declaration of the Rights of Man and Citizen," the manifesto of the French Revolution of 1789. This document states that "the aim of every political association is the preservation of the natural and inalienable rights of man. . . . [the] source of all sovereignty resides essentially in the nation; no group, no individual may exercise authority not emanating expressly therefrom. . . . [and] the law is the expression of the general will."[3] But in Hesse the "order" so highly vaunted by the legislative, executive, and judiciary minority had been expressly designed to reduce the people to a state of economic dependency and to rob the exploited of all vestiges of humanity. Büchner exposed the various governmental and bureaucratic departments as links in a chain strong enough to support the interests of the moneyed class and heavy enough to enslave the peasants. For example, the administration of justice has become the expression of "arbitrary will," not "law," for the people have lost all their human rights. "This justice is only a means to keep you in your place so that they can fleece you more easily."

Above all, Büchner detested hypocrisy and gave vent to his pent-up hatred in satire, disclosing human absurdity in all its pretensions. This literary weapon he directs against the main instigator of an inequitable society, the ducal house of Hesse. The ruler, who traditionally embodies the invulnerable sovereign, ordained to his majestic position by divine decree, is stripped bare of all the rich accoutrements of dress and royal guards. And what remains?—"a human being." This characterization Büchner justified in naturalistic terms. "He eats when he is hungry and sleeps when he grows tired." Physiologically speaking, Büchner could discover no differences between the ruler and the ruled since the former "crept as naked and weak into the world as [the people]." Büchner delighted in showing up man for what he really is, reducing him to that lowest stage of human life which we all share in common. Birth, death, nakedness, hunger, and sleep may all be said to designate the human animal, the level at which we all stand as equals, bereft of the artificial trappings of dress ("royal mantle"), society ("royal household"), or divine sanction ("his divine power").

As in Büchner's literary works, here, too, sex is recognized as an explosive social issue. Noble birth serves to vindicate and conceal debauched lives. "The royal mantle is the carpet upon which the noble gentlemen and ladies of the court roll over one another in their lewdness." Costly clothing meerly hides venereal diseases or corrupt and depraved minds and bodies while "the daughters of the people" are forced into prostitution by the ruling class. Once again what Büchner finds especially reprehensible is the hypocrisy, and the answer to it lies in a revelation of the true state of affairs.

The second thematic segment outlines the ideal form of government, derived primarily from the example offered by France. Constitutional monarchy is the goal. Being only the servant of the people, the king must be called upon to answer for his actions. All titles and rights of birth are to be abolished because "the highest power is in the will of all or of the majority." Since the legislative power must rest in the hands of a representative government elected by the people, the king will have only executive authority. Ultimately, Büchner believed, constitutional monarchy, an anachronism, would be replaced by a republic according to the French model. "Then the French got rid of the hereditary monarchy and freely elected a new government to which every nation has the right, according to reason and the Holy Scripture."

This ultimate aim is important from several points of view. It would appear on the surface that Büchner still preserved an optimistic belief that society could be transformed by means of revolution. The desired end—that of majority rule by the people—is one in which Büchner appeared to have faith at the time of writing. However, this faith was slated to be called into question and shaken drastically both before and during the composition of *Danton's Death*. Whereas the mention of the Bible may represent a concession to Weidig or the recognition of religion as a force equally instrumental in social revolution as "material wretchedness" eighteenth-century rationalism still remained at the heart of Büchner's insistence upon reason as the justification for a republican form of government.

The final section of *The Hessian Messenger* deals with a description of the reactionary movement in Europe, with special emphasis upon developments in France from Napoleon through Charles X and Louis Philippe. History is interpreted in terms of divine intervention and judgment. God clearly supported the ideals of the French Revolution, punishing the people with the restoration of monarchy for their refusal to adhere whole-heartedly to revolutionary goals (Weidig). In Germany the rulers reward and appease the people with constitutions that are "nothing but empty straw," while the provincial diets prove powerless in their attempts to place any effective check on the avarice of the princes. The dream of a German democracy has deteriorated into a wealth-oriented oligarchy. But if the people recognize that "no authority is ordained and blessed by God except that which is based upon the trust of the people and is elected specifically or tacitly by the people," then God will destroy the German tyrants by means of the people just as He destroyed Napoleon. This concept of God as architect of the historical process is obviously intended to appeal to the religiosity of the Hessian peasants. But Hesse constitutes only one limb of a body that will ultimately rise up from servitude to freedom, a signal for a revolution which will spread over the whole of Germany.

There is considerable evidence that Büchner's espousal of the unsuccessful uprising was a desperate last stand or a concession to his humanistic convictions, some of which he had already begun to doubt. As early as December 1832, he wrote to his family, "I have no more time for a political essay. It also would not be worth the effort; the whole thing is surely only a play." Later, from exile in Strasbourg, he acknowledged the futility of any individual action to effect political change, and the roots of this disillusionment can be found in his growing cynicism vis-à-vis human nature. Man naturally prefers the security of assured comfort and is not anxious to jeopardize his own welfare. "People will go into the fire if it comes from a burning punch bowl!" In a letter to the family dated February 1834, one cannot but detect a note of real pathos that will emerge more poignantly in his later literary production. "People call me a mocker. It's true that I often laugh, but I don't laugh at how someone is a human being but rather I laugh at the fact that he is a human being, for which he can't be blamed anyhow, and at the same time I laugh at myself, who share his fate." According to the report of a close acquaintance,[4] Büchner did not entertain any illusions about the peasants while writing *The Hessian Messenger*. "Thus it has come to the point that one must say despite all one's marked preference for [the peasants] that they have adopted a somewhat base attitude and that sadly enough they are susceptible almost only to an appeal made to their pocketbook." Büchner's grim view of man's fate was not only born out of a realistic approach to life but also out of a disillusion-ment with man himself, ruled as he is by his own selfish interests. Unfortunately, this low opinion of mankind was to be further confirmed by the actions of one of Büchner's coworkers, J. K. Kuhl, whose denunciation of the conspiracy led to the arrest of one of his friends. Returning to Giessen after a trip to warn his colleagues of the impending danger, Büch-ner discovered that his room had been searched. To divert suspicion from himself, he immediately pro-tested to the police against such illegal procedures. The police, on the basis of insufficient evidence, were unable to detain him.

The plan for a local rebellion ended in complete failure. As Büchner himself had foreseen, the peas-ants, accustomed to absolute obedience, surrendered the pamphlets to the authorities. Meanwhile, Weidig and many of his associates were imprisoned for trea-sonable action against the state. Fearing arrest and realizing that his complicity could not be concealed much longer, Büchner returned to Darmstadt. There, in his father's laboratory, he wrote his first play (*Dan-ton's Death*) in about four weeks, hoping to finance his escape from its sales. But before Karl Gutzkow, one of the leading figures of the Liberal Young Ger-many movement, could evaluate the work, Büchner wisely opted to cross the German border, arriving in Strasbourg in March 1835.

"Since crossing the border, I have a new source of energy; I now stand completely alone, but that in it-self increases my strength." In the relative security of political exile, Büchner immediately concentrated upon completing his study of philosophy and anatomy, having determined to abandon the career of a medi-

cal doctor for that of an academic. A letter written to his brother Wilhelm announces his decision to
renounce all political involvement as a result of his
realistic appraisal of the situation both in and outside
Germany. "I have been fully convinced for half a
year that nothing can be done and that anyone who
sacrifices himself at the present time is foolishly risk-
ing his life. . . . A close acquaintanceship with the
activities of the German revolutionaries in exile has
also convinced me that not the least can be expected
from this side." In addition to working on his doctoral
thesis "Mémoire sur le système nerveux du barbeau,"
he pursued his interest in literature, with the primary
intention of making some money on the side. He
translated into German two of Victor Hugo's plays,
Lucretia Borgia and *Maria Tudor*, and submitted his
only comedy *Leonce and Lena* to the Cotta publishing
house as part of a competition. The latter was returned unopened since the manuscript arrived two
days after the deadline. Also in 1836 he began to write
Woyzeck. A letter addressed to Gutzkow from Strasbourg bears witness to the fact that Büchner had not
renounced his compassionate concern for the people, a
love which surely dictated the composition of the first
German drama to deal with a protagonist from the
lower class. "I have become convinced that the educated and well-to-do minority, no matter how many
concessions it desires for itself from those in power,
will never want to give up its sarcastic relationship to
the biggest and most dispossessed class. And what
about this great dispossessed class itself? There are
only two levers capable of moving it: material wretchedness and religious fanaticism. Any party which
knows how to use these levers will win. Our times

need iron and bread—and then a cross or something like it."

After having received his doctor's degree from the University of Zurich and the offer of a position on its faculty, he moved to Zurich in October 1836, where he gave his inaugural lecture on cranial nerves. There are indications that while he gave his course in comparative anatomy, he continued working on the drafts of *Woyzeck*, and mention is also made in a letter of another play, *Pietro Aretino*, which has never been found. Early in 1837 an epidemic of typhus broke out in Zurich and by 2 February Büchner showed signs of having contracted this fatal disease to which he succumbed on 19 February 1837 before he had reached his twenty-fourth birthday.

2. BÜCHNER'S VIEW OF ART: *LENZ*

"Our Lord God has probably made the world as it is supposed to be, and we probably can't patch together anything better. Our one goal should be to copy him a little." This view of the artist as an imitator of God, a creator in his own right, was most probably adopted from the genius cult of the eighteenth-century "storm and stress" movement. The artist becomes the norm for the work of art, a law unto himself, since he alone is endowed with the insight and sensitivity necessary to assess his work. All critical appraisals by others are rejected as arbitrary and irrelevant. Büchner had subscribed to this concept, and his correspondence offers some evidence of his disdain for the critics of his era in their rejection of *Danton's Death* on moral grounds. However, Büchner has only scorn for the arrogant Promethean stance of the artist who wishes to rival the Deity, and against this Büchner proposes a mere continuation of the creative process in modesty and humility. Indeed, the supercilious, overconfident attitude of the genius-artist is exposed as illusionary through satirical means in *Leonce and Lena:*

VALERIO: Then let's become geniuses.

LEONCE: The nightingale of poetry sings the whole day above our heads, but the finest part goes to the devil unless we tear out its feathers and dip them in ink or paint.

In two major essays, "Fragments Concerning Recent German Literature" and "German Mentality and Art,"[1] Johann Gottfried Herder initiated a new form of literary criticism, the psychological-genetic method, to replace criteria derived from long-established aesthetic standards. His insistence on feeling one's way into the distinctive and unique identity of each work of art, which is viewed as an organic whole determined by and reflecting the character of an age, led to the view that art must be understood and appreciated as emerging from the particular ethos of its own period. Obviously aware of this approach, Büchner, as a high-school student, relied upon this principle to justify Cato's suicide.

Each age can offer us examples of such men, but all [of them] from time immemorial were subjected to the most diverse judgment. The cause of this is that each period applies *its* standard to the heroes of the present or past, that it does not judge according to the real value of these men [and] that its interpretation and judgment of these people are always determined and distinguished by the level upon which it itself stands. ... The lesson of this observation is: one must not judge the events and their effects according to how they reveal themselves *externally* but one must seek to establish their *inner deep meaning* and then one will find the *truth*.

Büchner's choice of models is also highly indebted to the "storm and stress" movement. "In a word, I have a high opinion of Goethe or Shakespeare, but a low one of Schiller." His veneration and imitation of the English playwright, part of a German tradition of "Shakespearemania" initiated by Herder's "Shakespeare" essay, has been well documented. Another source, the folk song, discovered and recognized as a literary genre by Herder, not only serves as a source of inspiration in *Lenz* but is utilized in *Woyzeck* to create atmosphere and to indirectly comment upon the action. Büchner, speaking in the persona of "storm and stress" dramatist Lenz, believed that Goethe only sometimes achieved that insight into life worthy of emulation—the early Goethe and not the Olympian figure with his classical serenity and aloofness—while Schiller is repudiated as the incarnation of idealism in art.

Büchner's most complete rejection of the "ideal poets" occurs in *Danton's Death*, where Camille acts as the dramatist's spokesman. If drama is not conventionalized to fit into the traditional mold, the public fails to comprehend or enjoy it. Art becomes static, predictable, and strictly regulated. It follows that "ideal poets" create puppets but not human beings of flesh and blood. "They hear and see nothing of the creation which glowing, rushing and shining is newly born around and in them every moment." This intensity must be sensed as something alive and vital, whereas idealizing art with its predilection for the artificial and the customary is by comparison defunct.

A true representation of reality, divorced from any attempt at transfiguration and defined in terms of nature, history, and life is the foremost demand Büchner makes of himself as an artist. "[I] draw my characters as I consider them in keeping with nature and history. . . ." Although being true to life implies the presentation of a *tranche de vie* (slice of life) regardless of moral issues, the creative writer occupies a position superior to that of the historian, as Büchner explains in a letter to his family. "The dramatic poet is in my eyes nothing more than a history writer but stands above the latter by virtue of the fact that he creates history for us a second time and immediately transposes us directly into the life of another time instead of giving a dry narrative; he gives us characters instead of characteristics and figures instead of descriptions." Far from composing a scientifically objective essay, the dramatist produces something alive and real which transfers the audience into another age.

Since Büchner attributes to lived reality a supreme value—one that encompasses the traditional categories of both the beautiful and the ugly—he refuses to recognize any convention in art other than a truthful reproduction of what *is*: "I demand in everything—life, possibility of existence, and then it's good. It is not for us to ask whether it is beautiful or whether it is ugly. The feeling that that which has been created has life stands above both of these considerations and is the only criterion in matters of art." In order to depict real life in its multifarious possibilities, the artist should seek to perpetuate moments pregnant with inner vitality. "The most beautiful pictures, the most swelling notes group together and dissolve. Only one thing remains: an endless beauty which steps from one form into another, eternally moving, changing. . . ." Forms mutate constantly and this process itself furnishes the true source of beauty. Although the artist's function is to give permanence to the moment, he must nonetheless recognize his limitations: "but of course one cannot always hold eternal beauty fast and put it in museums and reduce it to notes. . . ."

How is the artist to realize his goal? "Empathy" and "feeling," resulting in "impression" are the means towards the end. "One must love humanity in order to be able to penetrate into the real being of each person; no one should be too insignificant, no one too ugly. Only then can one understand humanity." The artist must love and feel his way into mankind if he ever hopes to portray its essence. "Just try it once," Büchner writes, "and sink yourself into the life of the least significant human being and reproduce this life in its palpitations, its intimations, in the whole subtle, scarcely noticed play of the features." Büchner does not advocate complete objectivity in the manner of the later realists, but the artist must nonetheless lose his own personality, possess the ability to delve into the individuality of another human being, and see the situation from this other point of view. If the poet requires empathy to create something true to life, nature, or history, the work of art itself must appeal above all to the reader's "feeling artery." We all have this ability to feel, "only the cover is more or less thick through which it must break." Art is therefore essentially a nonrational, emotional experience, which has to be felt from within. Classical art as entertainment for the mind is dismissed as untrue and invalid. "My favorite poet and sculptor is the one who gives me nature in its most realistic form so that I feel about his creation. . . ." Works born out of empathy and which give rise to intense feeling create a strong "impression," an emotional impact, that is subsequent to the recognition of authentic life. Büchner's Lenz ascribes a similar potential to the simple humanity of the New Testament episodes, to the faith of an old peasant woman, or to the Dutch masters.

In reference to *Danton's Death*, Büchner wrote: "It's a dramatic experiment and deals with material from recent history." Contemporary social reality, not a literary escape to the distant past, furnishes the major inspiration for Büchner's works. *Danton's Death*, carefully documented by references to and direct translations of historical records, takes place in the immediate past but, like *Leonce and Lena*, it also reflects the intellectual atmosphere at the beginning of the nineteenth century. *Lenz* is based to a large extent on the diary of Pastor Jean-Frédéric Oberlin, while *Woyzeck* takes its inspiration from the legal and medical disputes concerning the alleged insanity and subsequent execution of Johann Christian Woyzeck in the Leipzig market square on 27 August 1824.

The desire to remain true to history caused Büchner to portray the men of the French Revolution as "bloody, dissolute, energetic, and cynical." His preference for "the life of the least significant" as closest to the real man, the human animal, and his repudiation of high society, with its decorum and conventional attitudes which only obscure man's true nature, anticipate the naturalists' almost total preoccupation with the lower classes and the vulgar, sordid aspects of living. As Büchner demonstrates in *Woyzeck*, the lowest of men leads a more authentic existence. No longer should morality be a valid criterion for judging the merits of a work of art, because the artist cannot be more or less moral than history itself. True to his calling, Büchner depicts "Danton and the bandits of the revolution" not as "youthful heroes," but as historical figures characterized by "immorality," "ungodliness," and "obscene speech." "The poet is not a moral teacher, he invents and creates characters, he makes past times come alive again, and people can learn from this . . . what goes on around them in terms of human life." As creator, the poet presents the unadorned truth, and it is up to the individual to deduce any moral lessons from a work of art which exists for itself and not as a handbook on ethical behavior. If we insist upon ignoring the real world, it is tantamount to rejecting the Deity who created both the beautiful and the ugly, the good and the bad. "By the way, whenever people try to tell me that the poet must not show the world as it is but rather as it ought to be, I answer that I do not intend to make it better than God who certainly made the world as it ought to be."

From this analysis of Büchner's view of art, most of which he expressed through his alter ego Lenz in the short story of the same name, it becomes evident that Büchner demanded above all a faithful reproduction of reality. Having commenced a study of the German storm-and-stress dramatis Jakob Michael Lenz in 1835, he came upon the diary of Pastor Oberlin that described Lenz's stay at the minister's house in the Vosges Mountains. Availing himself of this historical record, Büchner created a narrative masterpiece. Because of the importance of *Lenz* both for its writer's general existential view and his concept of art, it would seem advisable at this point to take a brief look at his short prose work.

As he wanders through the mountains on his way to Waldbach, Lenz's mood swings from indifference to an hysterically intensified involvement with nature. He is suddenly gripped by panic which abates only when he reaches the house of Pastor Oberlin to whom he brings greetings from their mutual friend, Kaufmann. Oberlin warmly welcomes his visitor and expresses his pleasure at meeting Lenz, whose dramas he had enjoyed reading. The pastor invites him to stay and offers him a bed in the schoolhouse. That night, alone in his room, Lenz is overcome with an indefinable fear, to which he responds by inflicting bodily injury upon himself and which attains its climax when he runs outside into the dark and casts himself into the shallow well. To the astonished townspeople aroused by the splashing sound, he explains that he customarily takes a cold bath late at night.

The next morning, Lenz accompanies Oberlin on his rounds among his devoted parishioners. The serene day, however, is followed by a night beset by fears, and Lenz once again plunges himself into the water.

Having become accustomed to the simple way of life of Oberlin and his family, Lenz begins to show signs of being at peace with himself, of having found a religious solution to his personal dilemma. He then resolves to preach a sermon based on the theme of suffering as divine service. After the emotional experience of pouring out his feelings before the congregation, his mother appears to him in a dream symbolizing both love and death. But the idyllic peace of the valley community is disrupted for Lenz with the arrival of his friend, Kaufmann, who is the bearer of letters from Lenz's father urging him to return home. Lenz vehemently rejects Kaufmann's suggestion not to waste his life, exclaiming: "Away from here? Go home? To go mad there?"

At Kaufmann's suggestion Oberlin goes to Switzerland to see the theologian Lavater. Lenz accompanies the pastor part of the way and then roams the mountains on his lonely return journey. One night he chances upon a hut and spends the night there with a sick, delirious girl, an old woman who sings constantly, and a strange old man reputed to have supernatural powers. Still strangely restless, Lenz returns to Waldbach, where he seeks Madame Oberlin's company during the pastor's absence. The tranquil domestic atmosphere soothes his savage feelings, fears, and restlessness. One day a maid's song reminds him of his past unhappy love affair with Friederike. The memory tortures him, and he often talks about it to Madame Oberlin, who listens patiently but can do nothing to relieve his torment. When Lenz hears about the death of a child, named Friederike like his lost love, he becomes obsessed with the news. He fasts, smears his face with ashes—to Madame Oberlin's horror—and rushes, wrapped in an old sack, to the dead child's side. When he arrives, he grips the child's hand and praying feverishly commands: "Arise and walk!"—but the corpse remains cold. Lenz dashes out, blaspheming God. Exhausted, torn between deep religious feelings and revolt, he finally drags himself home.

As soon as Oberlin comes back from his visit to Lavater, he urges his guest to honor his father's wishes. Lenz begs the pastor not to cast him out and confesses his religious doubt. Oberlin reassures him. Suddenly he asks Oberlin what he knows about the girl. Oberlin, at a loss at to what Lenz means, asks for further particulars. Lenz rants on about Friederike and his mother, believing himself the murderer of both. His torments drive him to ask the pastor to scourge him and only the pastor's kindness and assurance of God's forgiveness quiet him temporarily. But at night he rushes once again through the courtyard, screaming

"Friederike," and throws himself into the little well. He then runs back to his room and out again to hurl himself once more into the water.

Oberlin, who is sincerely concerned about his charge's safety, sends for the schoolmaster, Sebastian Scheidecker, who, with his brother's aid, follows Lenz wherever he goes to prevent him from doing himself serious harm. Lenz escapes his overseers, however, and is finally discovered in a local home, where he had instructed the occupants to bind him with ropes after having denounced himself as a dangerous murderer.

Moods of relative calm and normalcy alternate with wilder and wilder expressions of insanity. Even Oberlin is powerless to help Lenz, who now hears voices. In an unguarded moment he jumps from the window in an attempt at suicide. Finally, in a mood of apathy and resignation, he is taken away in a wagon to Strasbourg. The demons are seemingly stilled, and he submits to an existence of emptiness, without desire, with life as just a necessary burden.

Upon reading this story for the first time, one cannot but be impressed by the skill and amazing powers of empathy evident in the recreation of Lenz's impression through striking, highly original diction. Although one is irresistibly drawn into the mind of a suffering human being, at the same time Büchner manages to provide an objective perspective by describing in almost clinical detail the psychological symptoms of a mental illness, hebephrenia, the commonest form of schizophrenia. "There was a quiver in his eyes and around his mouth, his clothes were torn." The victim becomes increasingly detached from reality, exhibits abnormal mannerisms, and gives evidence of indifference about personal appearance.

Schizophrenics also tend to lose control of their senses or confuse and misinterpret impulses sent to the brain. This dissociation can be readily ascertained in Lenz's fear of blindness, his impressions that his senses are failing him or that his limbs are growing weak. "However he complained a great deal about how heavy everything was, so heavy! He just couldn't believe that he would be able to walk."

"Now it seems to me so narrow, so narrow! Look, sometimes it seems to me as if I were pushing against the sky with my hands; oh, I'm suffocating! It seems to me at the same time as if I felt physical pain, here on the left side, in the arm with which I used to hold her."

Claustrophobia forces Lenz's retreat to the symbolic freedom and release of mountain-top panoramas. The further impression of pain underlines the extent to which the subconscious mind has gained power over the nerves and muscles normally controlled by the conscious mind. In addition to an increased sensual ambiguity, Lenz shows signs of heightened sensitivity resulting in hallucination. "Don't you hear anything? Don't you hear the terrible voice which screams around the whole horizon and which people usually call silence?"

Finally, in the closing stages of insanity, catatonic schizophrenia, a state of mental automatism in which the voluntary muscle systems keep any position in which they are put, manifests itself with a tyranny especially horrifying to Büchner. The individual is reduced to a marionette; the controlling strings become the innate instincts, not the mind. "What he did, he didn't do consciously, and yet an inner instinct compelled him." Büchner persistently returns to the image of the human puppet manipulated by inner forces and outer circumstances which he is powerless to direct.

In our first introduction to Lenz, we read, "He felt no fatigue, only he found it sometimes unpleasant that he couldn't walk on his head." This line is slipped in unobtrusively as part of a predominantly gray, depressive setting in a manner recalling to mind the matter-of-fact acceptance of surreality in a Kafka short story. Lenz desires to be able to transcend the banal, man's physical limitations, which render him incapable of walking on his head. Paranoic overtones become more explicit in the description of his self-identification with nature. "He felt a tear in his chest. He stood panting, his body bent forward, his eyes and mouth wide open, he thought he had to draw the storm into himself, contain everything in himself, he spread himself out and lay upon the earth, he burrowed himself into the universe, it was a pleasure which caused him pain."

One of the most consistently utilized word motifs within this short story is the term "fear." Nature, which enables Lenz to indulge his visions of grandeur, does not offer the tormented writer any form of fulfillment since it ultimately renders his awareness of solitude more poignant: "He felt dreadfully lonely; he was alone, completely alone." Fear may be conquered when the cause is known, but an ineffable one assumes terrifying proportions. "A nameless fear seized hold of him in this void: he was in emptiness!" Separation from human companionship leads man to think of himself and approach a paralyzing awareness of the absurdity of all human efforts, as is the case with Danton or Leonce. "[Lenz] was also afraid of himself in this solitude."

Fear assumes many forms in its relentless pursuit of the protagonist. Cut off from any meaningful link with an impersonal real world, Lenz becomes the victim of a persecution complex. "It was as if something were going after him and as if something terrible would have to get him, something which people can't stand, as if madness were chasing after him on horseback." The unknown enemy becomes an indefinite, intangible "something," the threat of insanity. Lenz, associating darkness with the void, isolation, and madness, finds the courage to bear his suffering solely in the light of day. "But only as long as the light lay in the valley was it bearable for him; toward evening a strange fear came over him, he would have liked to run after the sun." Lenz's greatest fear, that of isolation, expresses itself even physiologically: "he shook, his hair almost stood on end until he was exhausted under this most frightful strain." It finds its most vivid expression, however, in the visual image of the window utilized by Büchner on three separate occasions. When Lenz first enters Waldbach, he gazes through brightly illuminated windows and sees the happy faces of women and children. As an outsider, separated by a pane of glass, he is an observer and not a part of the human joy that glows within. Later, summarizing the solace and peace of mind he has achieved by his short stay in the Oberlin household, Lenz informs Kaufmann, "If I weren't able some time to go up a mountain and see the region and then go down again to the house, through the garden and look in through the window—I would go mad! mad!" Although he acknowledges his need of being able to look in upon the simple but good idyllic life of the country folk, he nonetheless persists in seeing himself as an exile who must content himself with a peripheral view of domestic happiness. Wandering through the mountains after the pastor's departure for Switzerland, Lenz discovers an alpine hut where the same visual motif is effectively and emphatically repeated for the third time: "He approached the window through which a shimmer of light fell." Outside, we are told, "it was a dark evening." Significantly, Lenz is part of this outer darkness, implying the black solitude of isolation verging on despair. The illuminated hut becomes synonymous with peace of mind, acceptance of an uncomplicated way of life, and above all the inner security of the home, which Lenz, as a mere observer, will never enjoy.

We thus sense Lenz's awareness of his growing alienation from society and the desire to penetrate through the window to become part of the human community within. The movement proceeds from the cold exterior to a warm interior. However, in Lenz's last act, the order is reversed. Casting himself out the window, a final confirmation of his insanity, Lenz symbolically and physically breaks through the barrier, but in the wrong direction. The fall suggests the collapse of any faith in the healing power of human companionship and resignation to the cold despair of external isolation.

"It seemed to him as if old figures, forgotten faces were again stepping out of the dark, old songs were awakened, he was away, far away." Very early in the narrative it is intimated that Lenz is a man with a heavy past, a past which he fears since it weighs heavily upon him. His experiences prior to the events of the story are centered around two women. The first, his mother, is closely associated in his mind with nature: "he sometimes thought that his mother would have to step out from behind a tree, as big as life, and tell him that she had granted to him all this [winter landscape]." Although an authoritative figure, it is implied that she is a loving person, who displays genuine concern for her son. The most important note is, therefore, that of human affection which Lenz so desperately craves.

The second, an unknown female character, at first only "a figure which always hovered before his eyes," continually preoccupies Lenz's imagination. During the night in the alpine hut, he is captivated by some mysterious power emanating from the delirious girl's features in the moonlight. The note of anguish upon her face the next morning—"she now had an expression of indescribable suffering"—heightens a sense of past recollection. The maid's song: "Upon this earth I have no joy, I have my darling but he's far away" also conjures up a distant memory. True happiness can be realized only through the establishment of human relationships, such as mother to child, husband to wife, or man to woman. The historical Lenz attempted unsuccessfully to establish a liaison with Friederike Brion in the parsonage at Sesenheim after Goethe had left her. The song consequently represents a cruel reminder of an unfortunate love affair. "God, you are still the only people where I could put up with it, and yet—yet, I must go, to her—but I cannot, I may not."

"When she used to go through the room like that and sang by herself like that half for herself and every step was music, there was such bliss in her and that flowed over into me; I was always calm when I looked at her or she leaned her head on me like that." A visual image only recently impressed upon the psyche has become inextricably linked with reminiscences of past happiness. The reference to the female head leaning on Lenz most likely refers to Friederike Brion, while the singing recalls to the reader's mind the mad girl of the mountain hut. Lenz is quite obviously confusing his Friederike episode with the more recent encounter with the deranged young girl. "But I can't imagine her, the image runs away from me and this tortures me."

"Oh, is she dead? Is she still living? The angel! She loved me—I loved her, she was worthy of it—oh, the angel! Cursed jealousy. I have sacrificed her—she still loved another man—I loved her, she was worthy of it—oh mother dear, she also loved me—I'm your murderer!" Friederike Brion and the mother have joined forces to accuse Lenz's sick mind and remind it of its guilt. Through lack of faith he has murdered them. The past has succeeded in catching up with him. Oberlin and Waldbach were only temporary escapes from the persecutions of his prior life. "Lenz ran through the courtyard, called with a hollow, hard voice the name Friederike, pronounced with the utmost speed, confusion, and despair."

Once Lenz has convinced himself of some form of guilt—be it the result of his inability to raise the child from the dead, his blasphemy against God, or his jealousy which terminated his liaison with Friederike Brion—he wants to be punished. Oberlin refuses to scourge him, insisting that Christ's sacrifice has paid for all his sins. But hoping to gain absolution through self-imposed penitence and seeking to alleviate his destructive meditations, he throws himself out the window.

Death in *Lenz*, in contrast to *Danton's Death* or *Leonce and Lena* where it is actively sought after or

longed for, serves primarily to create a general atmosphere of disillusionment and despair. At one point
Lenz feels empty, cold, and dying, an indication of a
gradual emotional death. Even suicide, only half-
heartedly attempted, does not offer a valid alternative,
because "for him there was of course no peace and
hope in death." It ironically becomes a means "to
bring him back to himself through physical pain."
Man is made aware of his existence, of his being alive,
through suffering.

Nature provides Lenz initially with a meaningful
escape from the limitations of civilized life. Above all,
he delights in retiring to mountain tops where he is
overcome by a sensation of omnipotence and release
equal in vastness to the panorama before his eyes.
Nature also possesses some mysterious, primordial
energy with which he seeks communion. The mountain people, unspoiled by contact with urban centers,
develop a close, intimate rapport with physical forces.
"The simplest, purest form of nature [is] most closely
related to the elementary form of nature; the more
subtly man feels and lives intellectually, the more this
elementary sense becomes dulled." The more rationally oriented one becomes, the less one is able to feel
the essence of nature. This "elementary sense," we are
told, is not necessarily a higher state since the natural
forces have a demonic dimension which controls the
individual, but it nonetheless offers the recipient "an
eternal feeling of joy" because he becomes one with
nature and thus shares the special life of each animal,
vegetable, or mineral. Büchner clearly recognizes an
independent power beyond the rational. Man is capable of feeling or sensing this power when he returns to
a more primitive relationship with the life force from

which he evolved. On the other hand, the intellect, the basis of civilization, distinguishes, separates, and divides, thus diminishing this sense of association.

Whereas nature at first comforts and strengthens the young man, it eventually turns against him to become a source of fear. This complete reversal in clinical terms constitutes an additional manifestation of a persecution mania where everything appears as hostile to the individual. "[The] landscape frightened him, it was so narrow that he feared to bump against everything."

Lenz's attempt at a Rousseauesque return to the society of country people represents an alternative means of escape. Idyllic scenes of patriarchal simplicity, faith, and security have a peaceful effect upon the poet. "[The] snug room and the quiet faces which stood out from the shadow: the bright faces of children upon which all the light appeared to rest and which gazed up curiously, confidently towards mother who sat quietly like an angel in the shadow behind." This idealized vision leads to a sense of belonging: "immediately he was at home." The local inhabitants are also closely attuned to nature, for which their respect verges on worship. "The people, silent and serious, as if they didn't dare disturb the peace of their valley, extended a quiet greeting as they rode past." But country life and human society prove equally ineffective as Lenz, in the final stages of his illness, flees all human companionship with the exception of Oberlin.

As the village pastor, Oberlin has gained the love and trust of the people who seek his advice on vital matters. He embodies a simple but sincere faith, which expresses itself in part through practical work, such as staking out new roads or visiting schools. This combination of genuine Christian piety and involvement in the everyday tasks of living offers an uncomplicated way of life guaranteeing the peace of mind for which Lenz craves. "Everything had a salutary and soothing effect on him." As Lenz becomes increasingly enveloped in Oberlin's routine, he shows less evidence of being agitated. "But the more he became accustomed to this life, the calmer he became."

"Yes, I can't stand it; do you intend to reject me? Only in you is the way to God. But it's all over for me! I have fallen from the path, damned for all eternity, I'm the eternal Jew." Above all, Lenz fears rejection by Oberlin, the incarnation of true Christianity. He senses that the pastor represents his last contact with the Christian solution to the enigma of life—unshakable faith. But religion fails to assuage a tormented mind damned with the fate of Ahasuerus, the wandering Jew.

The one irreplaceable goal of Lenz's yearning, whether it be sought in nature, idyllic village life, or human companionship, is peace of mind. Suffering from essentially the same *mal du siècle* as Danton or Leonce, an illness which in the poet's case has assumed pathological proportions, Lenz observes that "everyone needs something; if he can be at peace, what more could he have! To climb continually, to struggle, and thus to throw away eternally everything which the moment offers, and continually to go without in order to enjoy just once! To thirst while bright springs gush across one's path!" Life consists of constant struggle and insatiable ambition, leading man to mount upward towards dissatisfaction and to fail to appreciate the wealth of each moment. The inherent drive to enjoy, one which is fated never to be fully satisfied, is at the basis of all human activity. This insight on the part of Lenz renders peace of mind the most cherished goal man may achieve and anticipates the final note of resignation since peace of mind is diametrically opposed to "climbing" and "struggling," the essence of the absurd treadmill of daily existence.

The subject of Lenz's sermon delivered to the community of Waldbach is suffering, and the object, to bring peace to the people's hearts. Life on earth corresponds to the traditional vale of tears of material hardship, while suffering, according to Christian teaching, leads us to heaven.

> "Let the holy pains, like deep wells,
> Burst forth wholly within me;
> Let suffering be all my gain,
> Let suffering be my divine service."

Pain has positive value here, for it makes man more aware of himself and his hidden potential. In suffering we achieve mercy and salvation; we serve God by accepting through faith the suffering He imposes upon us. "For him [Lenz] the universe was wounded; he felt deep inexpressible pain because of this." As a result of the existence of evil, man must suffer for the imperfections of the world.

"Then he implored that God might give him a sign." Subsequent to Lenz's meeting with the saint of the alpine hut, he expresses the desire to become a similar prophet. God must perform a miracle to prove his mission and subdue his doubt. The death of a child, significantly another Friederike in nearby Fouday, offers Lenz the first opportunity to essay his new ministry. When he sees the child with its cold, glassy eyes, he witnesses his own isolation and lack of warmth. "The child seemed to him so forsaken and he himself so alone and lonely." The fact that the young girl's features will soon decay causes Lenz "violent pain," for a child's misery seems to the adult mind especially unmerited. Asking God to restore his faith by granting him divine power, Lenz even goes as far as to assume Christ's role. "[He] prayed with all the distress of despair that God perform a sign in him and revive the child . . . 'Arise and walk!' " But the cadaver remains cold and lifeless; and Lenz, feeling totally betrayed and abandoned, revolts against a god who denies him consolation. "The sky was a stupid blue eye, and the moon stood quite ridiculously in the middle of it, foolishly. Lenz had to laugh aloud, and with this laugh, atheism seized him and held him quite securely and calmly and tightly." Rejection of God is again born out of the question: "Why do I suffer?" This realization together with a loss of faith manifests itself in a view of life as meaningless and absurd. "For him everything was empty and hollow."

"But I, if I were omnipotent, look here, if I were thus, I would not be able to bear the suffering, I would save, save; I want nothing but peace, peace, only a little peace in order to be able to sleep." If God loves his creation, why does He not mitigate our lot of pain as Lenz would do were he God? Why does God allow him to suffer the way he does? Surely, through the lips of a poet driven insane by a life of mental pain and persecution, this statement constitutes Büchner's most poignant expression of his own personal obsession and dilemma, the issue of human suffering which constitutes the unifying theme of *The Hessian Messenger* and the three plays.

"He sat in the wagon with cold resignation as they drove out of the valley toward the west." The only attitude possible in Büchner's world is one of resignation or indifference. "It was all the same to him where they took him . . . he was completely indifferent. . . . He did everything as the others did; but there was a terrible emptiness in him, he no longer felt fear, had no desire, his existence was for him a necessary burden. Thus he lived on. . . ." *Lenz* remains perhaps the most logically consistent of all of Büchner's literary works since the ultimate fate of its protagonist represents the inevitable solution for a writer when everything is "empty and hollow," especially if there is no female love to fill the void. Life becomes a necessary burden which only the fear of death, the final escape, prevents man from casting aside.

3. *DANTON'S DEATH*

Since the French Revolution broke out in 1789, almost five years have passed and the struggle for power continues in the declining days of the Reign of Terror. Hébert and his extreme faction have been sent to the guillotine. There now remains a forced coalition of the Dantonists, who, led by Georg Danton, advocate moderation and liberalism, and of the more radical Jacobins, who, supported by the rhetoric and views of their leader Robespierre, stand for the bloody continuation of the Revolution. The dramatization of twelve days in 1794 (March 24–April 5) reveals the inevitable clash between the two parties and the subsequent downfall and death of Danton and his followers. From the first scene it becomes apparent that the active revolutionary Danton, who ordered the September Massacre and saved the Revolution, has been reduced to a passive observer, a man who has seen into the abyss of human existence and has been permanently lamed by his insight. Thus he fails to take seriously the warnings of Camille and Philippeau, while Robespierre, the Messiah of the people, demonstrates his control over the masses and in the Jacobin

Club declares war against the "immoral." This amounts to an attack leveled at Danton, who is subsequently found at the feet of a Palais-Royal prostitute. A confrontation between Robespierre and Danton finally convinces the latter that he should act. But overcome by boredom, persuaded of the ineffectiveness of individual action before the tyrannical forces of the Revolution, he resorts to the rationalization "They won't dare" and refuses to flee even though he has been informed that orders have been issued for his arrest. Danton reveals to his wife the sense of helpless despair and persecution which has determined his anti-heroic stance. "We are puppets drawn on a string by unknown powers; we ourselves are nothing, nothing!" Robespierre has Danton and his followers arrested and successfully defends this action before the National Convention. A discussion conducted by prisoners in the Luxembourg as to the existence or non-existence of God establishes the philosophical basis for the cynical, nihilistic atmosphere which permeates the drama. Brought before a donkey court of the Revolutionary Tribunal, Danton regains his old rhetorical power and in a devastating attack against his enemies wins the enthusiastic support of the spectators. However, the disclosure of an alleged plot to release Danton from jail by force gives his enemies the necessary excuse to expedite the trial. As an effective contrast to the macabre, depressing prison conversations and the corrupt, mechanical, bureaucratic procedure of the court that ends with Danton's execution, the play offers moving personal scenes surrounding Julie, Danton's wife, who out of love and loyalty to her husband poisons herself, and Lucile, Camille's wife, who occupies the center of the stage in the last two scenes.

Driven to the point of insanity by the loss of her husband, she sits down on the steps of the guillotine. As a patrol passes, she cries out "Long live the King!" and thus effectively signs her own death warrant.

One of the most consistent themes of modern literature has been the breakdown in human communication. In the first scene of *Danton's Death*, Julie asks her husband, "Do you believe in me?" Mutual faith is one of the main requirements of true love, but the very necessity of verbal assurance indicates an element of doubt. Danton replies: "We know little about one another." Even among lovers, it remains impossible to break down the barriers which separate us. We are all cursed with thick, hence insensitive skins, but nonetheless in despair "we stretch out our hands to one another" in response to a congenital need for understanding and warmth. Because all physical attempts to achieve rapport fail to reach the emotional or real human being within, "we are very lonely." The isolation of man was to remain a dominant image in all of Büchner's subsequent works.

What constitutes knowing an individual, Danton ponders. What really goes on in the mind of the one opposite and can we ever hope to penetrate through sensual limitation to attain the essence within? "Forget it, we have rough senses. Know one another? We would have to break open our skulls and tear the thoughts out of each other's brain fibers." Our senses, the sole source of our ideas and sentiments, are too coarse. Since all our emotions and mental activity depend upon sensory perception, man remains exceptionally limited and determined by his "rough senses."

One of the major consequences of the discovery of

sensory determinism was to place man into the natural realm as a more highly developed organism but nonetheless subject to the immutable laws governing the cosmos. Some of the principles affecting the evolving forms of life are now commonly acknowledged, such as the theory of natural selection or the survival of the fittest. Nature is viewed as a cruel mother who destroys those of her offspring who do not possess either the physical or mental prowess to stay alive. At each stage of development, certain species were eliminated to make way for a more advanced stage. The French Revolution as portrayed by Büchner with its continual executions and struggle for power, represents a political as well as a social jungle where the law of survival is simply kill or be killed. It is exemplified in the earlier case of the radical Hébert and his supporters or in the conflict between the Dantonists and the Jacobins. "The Revolution is like Saturnus, he eats his own children."

The most far-reaching effect of the evolutionary or materialistic approach in the field of drama is the denial of free will, which is the basic assumption of classical tragedy. In one of the more terrifying scenes of the play, Danton, haunted by remorse for having instigated the September Massacre, seeks to appease his conscience. "Yes, I did it, it was self-defense, we had to." History pressed him into a position where force was the only solution. "The Man on the cross made it easy for himself." To relinquish one's life barely constitutes a real sacrifice but may indeed be a subtle form of self-indulgence, the "sensual pleasure of pain" as Robespierre defines it. But to be obliged to abandon one's peace of mind, to do what one knows is basically evil to avert a worse evil, this is true self-immolation.

"[For] it must needs be that offenses come; but woe to that man by whom the offense cometh!" While the historical process demands violence and suffering to achieve social transformation, it shows no mercy to the agents or the victims through whom the change is brought about. Circumstances, history, perhaps even a god, have singled man out to perform a nefarious deed for which he must bear the physical and even more painful psychological consequences. "Who will curse the hand upon which the curse of the 'must' has fallen?" On the basis of this deterministic view, a moral judgment can not be passed; good and bad, reward and punishment are no longer meaningful terms.

Another recurring image indicative of man's lack of free will appears in the recognition of existence as subject to an indifferent mechanism. "But it seems to me as if I had fallen into the works of a mill and my limbs were being slowly, systematically twisted off by the cold physical power. To be killed so mechanically!" Danton is so obsessed with the illusion that a physical force is automatically and irrevocably destroying him that even dying represents no new experience, no escape from the humdrum of everyday life. Man is a mere cog in a gigantic wheel. Once it is set in motion, the insignificant cog must perform its task to insure the clock-work regularity and uniformity of the whole. Since Danton is fully aware of the rule of necessity, which the individual can only ascertain but not exploit for the well-being of himself or humanity, he now surrenders himself to negative musing and meditation. The positive intention of the idealist, formerly translated into deeds, has been irrevocably crippled. Just as Büchner in that fateful letter to his fiancée achieved the shattering insight into the "fatalism of history," in like manner Danton has recognized the complete futility of individual action and has pessimistically resigned himself to the inevitable.

"A mistake was made as to how we were created. We are lacking something. I have no name for it. . . . What is it that lies, whores, steals and murders in us?" Why was man not created in a more perfect form, and why must evil remain an integral part of his psychologic make-up? The missing component cannot be named, but without it, we continually fail to achieve any permanent good. Therefore war and execution have lost their value for a man of Danton's insight, for they remain ineffective in transforming human nature. "But we shall not root it out of one another's intestines; why therefore should we break open one another's bodies?"

Although Danton is unable to specify the nature of the "mistake," a close examination soon reveals a possible cause of man's deficiency. "There are only Epicureans, and specifically, coarse and subtle ones; Christ was the most subtle; that is the only difference that I can ascertain between human beings. Everyone acts according to his nature, i.e., he does that which gives him pleasure." As Danton explains to Robespierre, the refined or educated seek intellectual pleasure whereas the more lowly indulge in physical gratification. Pleasure may be obtained from art, self-abnegation, or even suffering for the sake of one's convictions. We are all destined to follow our most dominant drive, to seek our own welfare, and by so doing, we become the unwitting victims of a psychological determinism. Even religion is relegated to the realm of self-interest. In the words of the prostitute

Marion, "it all depends on one thing, from where one gets one's pleasure, from bodies, pictures of Christ, flowers, or children's toys: it's the same feeling; he who enjoys the most, prays the most." Since all men are motivated by the pleasure principle, sex and religion are only different aspects of the same basic selfishness.

The personality of Robespierre offers an intriguing and highly perceptive character study of a man obsessed with the concept of virtue and his vision of grandeur as the savior of the people. High ethical standards have become an effective weapon enabling Robespierre to exploit the Revolution as an instrument of revenge on the whole of humanity. In the confrontation between the perverted idealist, Robespierre, and the pragmatic epicurean, Danton, virtue is exposed as a sustaining illusion, an escape from cruel reality. Robespierre's financial solvency, his self-imposed chastity, and proper dress reflect superficial and hypocritical social standards that have enabled him to camouflage his true personality, the human animal with its self-centered impulses. Robespierre, the apparent paragon of honesty, is only a subtle epicurean whose pleasure lies in maintaining an unnatural moral code in order to look down upon those who live a more authentic existence. As Danton points out to Robespierre, "I would be ashamed to run around between heaven and earth for thirty years with the same morally self-righteous look only for the sake of the wretched pleasure of finding others worse than myself. Is there nothing in you which sometimes tells you quite softly, secretly: you're lying, you're lying!?"

Once Danton has left the stage, Robespierre, vulnerable to his rival's attack on his morality, assesses his motives in an amazing monologue. The suppressed drives and emotions of an ascetic find release in an erotically colored fantasy. "Thoughts, wishes, scarcely suspected, confused and formless, which shyly crept away from the light of day, now receive shape and form and steal into the silent house of dream. They open doors, they look out of windows, they become to a certain extent flesh, limbs stretch in sleep, lips murmur." The scene culminates in the statement: "Verily, the son of man is crucified in all of us; we all struggle in the Garden of Gethsemane in bloody sweat, but no one saves the other with his wounds." Here Robespierre gives evidence of the same perception which has paralyzed Danton's will to act. A pathetic figure, worthy of some sympathy, Robespierre recognizes the senselessness of his strivings and the futility of wishing to save mankind. All attempts to create heaven on earth will fail since we are victims of fate. Torn by his sincere affection for Camille, the one man who befriended and loved him as a boy, he nonetheless must kill him or be killed. A typical Büchnerian protagonist, he stands ultimately alone, bereft of all human companionship. "They're all leaving me—everything is desolate and empty—I'm alone."

In turning from the leaders of the Revolution to the people, there is even less cause for optimism. Motivated by pure selfishness, the mob is governed by the basic drives of the human animal: food, shelter, and sex; and its members show concern only for the personal advantages they may derive for themselves from a given situation. Since they have been reduced to rapacious animals, they live by the rule of survival and destroy without any hesitation all who dare stand in their way. "The people are a minotaur that weekly must have its corpses if it's not to eat up [those in power]." The incident with the young man who by his wit saves himself from hanging is indicative of mob rule where life is cheap and law and order impossible. Individuals are executed at the mere whim of the masses. The law, according to Robespierre, is the will of the people, but this will desires that there be no law, only anarchy, a return to the jungle where the conventions and standards that assure the foundations of civilization are nullified.

One of the Dantonists, Lacroix, observes, "The people are virtuous, that is to say they don't enjoy, because work has made their sensual organs dull. They don't get drunk because they have no money, and they don't go into the brothel because their breath stinks of cheese and herring and makes the girls want to throw up." The people's moral standards are born out of economic necessity or lack of opportunity. Because they have nothing and a life of immorality demands wealth and leisure, they are forced to abstain. It follows that the masses' hatred of the sensualists, i.e., Danton and his colleagues, originates in envy; for they would also like to indulge themselves. Thwarted, they must resort to hatred. "The people hate the sensualists as an eunuch hates men." Robespierre's apparent faith in the people is not in any way substantiated by their role within the play. Büchner's more realistic portrayal reveals a low form of subservience, the result of a long tradition of degrading obedience, which is difficult to overcome. In the words of a Jacobin, "The people have an instinct to let themselves be kicked." And finally their vacillating nature is underlined in a street scene which begins, "Down with the Decemvirs! Long live Danton!" Jealousy, derived from a comparison of the sensuality of Danton with the austerity of "the virtuous Robespierre," leads to a complete reversal of the initial outcry, and the episode terminates, "Long live Robespierre! Down with Danton! Down with the traitor!"

"I [Danton] sense something in the atmosphere; it's as if the sun were hatching fornication." The sexually explosive atmosphere that permeates *Danton's Death* shocked Büchner's contemporaries. Of course, the use of the vulgar and the obscene as comic relief was not unknown to an admirer of Shakespeare. However, the excessive depiction of the erotic not only supplies humor but also is associated with the more serious, pessimistic side of the drama. "On the street there were dogs, a mastiff and a small Bolognese lap dog which were trying their best to copulate. . . . Flies do it on your hands; that leads to ideas." The animal world openly responds to the sexual drive, and copulation becomes a common sight on any city street. Whereas dogs and insects naturally follow their instincts, society has forced the human animal, plagued with the same desire, to conceal or suppress them behind an unnatural, repressive moral code.

In addition, sex represents a desperate attempt to transcend physical limitations and become united with the object of one's passion. "Why can't I [Danton] completely grasp your [Marion's] beauty within me, completely surround it? . . . I would like to be a part of the air in order to bathe you in my flow, in order to break myself on each wave of your beautiful body." In the desire to encompass within himself Marion's beauty, Danton discloses again his craving for close contact. To be totally consumed by another individual, to lose one's identity, is to strive for communi-

cation through love. Submerged in a Dionysiac experience, Danton forgets his individual predicament.
When, however, he is called back into the conscious
world of political dangers and human cruelty, the
warmth and protective shield of erotic love are soon
dissolved. Marion says: "Your [Danton's] lips have
grown cold, your words have suffocated your kisses."
Sex offers only a temporary release from reality into
illusion.

"Julie, I love you like the grave," says Danton.
Death also provides peace of mind, a retreat from
horrifying mental preoccupations. Love leads to a
temporary loss of individual consciousness and this is
precisely what Danton longs for: rest from the bitter
reproaches of his conscience, a form of psychological
escape from an unbearable existence. "O Julie! If I
were to go alone! If she were to leave me alone!—And
if I were to decay completely, disintegrate completely,
I would be a handful of tortured dust, each one of my
atoms could only find peace beside her." The terror of
death lies in the fear of being irrevocably cut off from
all human warmth. In considering death, Danton looks
for solace solely in Julie. Thus, in a predominantly
black vision there is nonetheless one ray of warmth
and hope—woman. The female types in Büchner's
works seem to descend from one and the same prototype, Marion, a study of the natural woman who is
even more naive and simpler than Goethe's Gretchen,
her possible model. Innocent and wholesome as a
child, she has no preconceived notions of good and
evil. It is society which imposes these arbitrary values
on its citizens. Since man is not born with an innate
moral understanding, her only guide other than her
mother, is her natural impulses. In a sense she becomes

one with the spring whose arrival heralds the sexual awakening of the adolescent. "Then the spring came; something was happening all around me in which I had no share. I ended up in a strange atmosphere, it almost suffocated me." As a child of nature, Marion displays an intimate association with the physical world, and this further emphasizes the basic notion of a human animal living in harmony with the natural sphere from which it evolved. "I sank into the waves of the evening sunset." As with her sexual experience, Marion is totally absorbed in nature and becomes identified with the physical forces which attract her in an irresistible manner. Sex, however, assumes such a tyrannical control of her life that she knows of no change and becomes, like Danton, a mechanism caught up in a process over which she has no control. "I am always only one, an uninterrupted yearning and grasping, a fire, a stream." If the story of Marion is taken to its logical conclusion, we must assume that Büchner recognized the danger in any absolute return to nature as a guiding principle.

The poet Byron once wrote that "Man's love is of man's life a thing apart,/'Tis woman's whole existence."[1] This applies not only to Marion but to Lucile and Julie as well. The world simply does not exist beyond the object of Lucile's affection—Camille. In the great simplicity and in the immense sincerity of her love, she fails to comprehend why anyone should wish to destroy her little realm. "The world is wide and there are many things in it—but why then [Camille's head]? Who'd want to take it from me? That would be wicked. And what do they intend to do with it?" Defenseless and extremely vulnerable in a hostile order of existence which she cannot comprehend, she must resort to resignation and finally insanity. Very little difference can be ascertained in the characterization of Lucile and Julie. Totally unintellectual, ruled by emotion, and incapable of understanding the political situation or their husbands, Lucile and Julie are nonetheless amazingly generous with their compassionate love. Julie's dominant feature remains her total devotion to Danton. A self-negating love, it transcends man's greatest fear, that of death, and contradicts man's strongest instinct, the will to survive.

Danton's Death would appear to support a decidedly negative view of man as an egocentric animal who utilizes his superior rational faculties to better his own position at the expense of others. If one were to exclude the female characters, this picture would indeed be most bleak if it were not for the important note of "mercy" rendered by Danton and his associates. Compassion for the numerous victims of the revolution led Camille and Danton to advocate moderation and the end of all executions, but in so doing they paved the way for their own extinction: "I [Camille] go to the scaffold because my eyes filled with tears at the fate of some wretched souls." Earlier in the drama Danton states, "I would rather be guillotined than to allow others to be guillotined. I'm sick of it; why should we human beings fight with one another? We ought to sit down beside one another and have peace and quiet." Appalled by the loss of life in the name of the revolution and filled with a sincere love for humanity, Danton refuses to be the instrument of further oppression.

After a long philosophical discussion designed to demonstrate the nonexistence of God, Payne maintains, "One can deny evil but not pain; only the mind can prove the existence of God; feeling revolts against it. . . . Why do I suffer? That is the cliff of atheism." Whereas human reason may logically prove that there is a God, human feeling finds it difficult to accept the concept of a loving, just Father. When man faces this dilemma arising from the irrational, his self-esteem, derived from his intellectual capabilities, breaks down. "The slightest quiver of pain, and even if it were to occur in only one atom, makes a tear in creation from the top to the bottom."

The immediate response to the issue of human suffering is Danton's rejection of existence. "The world is chaos. The void is the world god to be born." Traditionally the earth was supposed to have been formed out of chaos by a regulating force, but here creation is reversed. The world equals chaos because no rationally discernible principle determines life on earth. Since existence is meaningless and its absurdity only serves to crucify the minds and hearts of men, it would be better if all that existed were destroyed. This point of view partially explains Danton's statement: "I shall know how to die courageously; it's easier than living." Death appears to be the only solution. "The void will soon be my refuge;—life is a burden to me; people may tear it away from me; I long to shake it off."

And yet, in a complete reversal of position, disillusionment and resignation, with decidedly nihilistic overtones, turn into a passionate craving for life and an overwhelming fear of death. In Danton's final speeches before the Revolutionary Tribunal, we no longer hear the words of a man who longs for death, but an ardent, fiery defense of an individual fighting for survival. "The voice of a man who is defending his honor and his life must shout louder than your [court official's] bell." How then do we explain this apparent contradiction? Where does Danton find the strength and justification for continuing an existence which he himself has characterized as wretched? "O Julie! If I were to go alone! . . . I can't die, no I can't die."

The affection between two human beings sounds a brief life-affirming note in this requiem to a revolution. Danton's last act is an attempt to receive the embrace of his friend Hérault, which is thwarted by the executioner. "Do you [the executioner] mean to be crueller than death? Can you prevent our heads from kissing one another at the bottom of the basket?"

Leonce and Lena was not produced until 1885, and *Danton's Death* had to wait no less than sixty-five years after Büchner's death for its first public performance. Several explanations may be proposed for this late recognition: the predominance of German idealism and its optimistic belief in human progress and in the positive action of an individual hero; Büchner's often total disrespect or disregard for the literary conventions of his age, and consequently his seemingly radical innovations in style, structure, and subject matter. However, an histrionic sixth sense led him to create two tragedies and one comedy which have been viewed as precursors of nearly every significant dramatic development from naturalism to the "theatre of the absurd."

Danton's Death has consistently been a very problematic work both in staging and in interpretation. Stylistically it represents a revolt against classicism in its preference for prose over traditional verse. Büchner's refusal to accommodate idealism in art results in a concrete, down-to-earth language, often employing crude images to depict the ugly, repulsive, animalistic side of life. Even in the twentieth century, it has been found advisable to delete the more blatant obscenities. But, above all, the open-ended structure of a play containing thirty-two scenes, each of which could be considered complete in itself and not necessarily sequential, has presented directors with the headache of perpetual set changes. The three unities have been discarded, the division into four acts seems a matter of convenience only and most of the scenes (one consists of a mere five lines!) tend to retard rather than promote the action. And yet *Danton's Death* does exhibit a fundamental form based on contrast. An essentially lyrical, personal moment is juxtaposed with the harsh reality of a mob scene. Short scenes, often combined in the interest of expediency, tend to be more functional in nature, preparing for the numerous long monologues which Büchner indulges in to disclose an inner state of mind. Despite the languid, almost static impression with which the play leaves the audience, the plot progresses slowly but surely towards its inevitable conclusion in the guillotine, which in some productions has occupied the center of the stage from the very outset.

This open form has given directors a great range of interpretation between the two poles of the masses and the individual. Preference for either one has frequently resulted in harm to the other, and almost inevitably the choice was dictated by the political or social preoccupations of the age, not by a need to be true to the author's intentions. But this in itself supplies further evidence of Büchner's inexhaustible appeal to the most divergent groups in the twentieth century.

The first attempt to put this unwieldy giant on stage occurred on 5 January 1902 at an afternoon performance offered by a local club in the Berlin Belle-Alliance Theater. A critic of the *Tag* remarked: "Although it was a case of an experiment with completely inadequate means because the difficulties which arise in the staging of Büchner's drama are much too big for a club stage to be able to cope with . . . nonetheless the experiment was rewarded with lively applause."[2] To judge from other reports, it was a totally unacceptable production plagued with poor acting. In fact, Else Schiff, who only accepted the role of Lucile at the last moment, was heralded as the most outstanding performer.

On 8 November 1913, Dr. Eugen Kilian directed an important public performance of *Danton's Death* together with the première of *Woyzeck* in the Munich Residenztheater on the occasion of the 100th anniversary of Büchner's birth. While avoiding the temptation of presenting a revolutionary play, Kilian, aided by Karl Wolff, the dramatic consultant, endeavoured to portray the mood of the intimate scenes, and the wider revolutionary dimension of the play. "A simple system of curtains and a few movable sets and backcloths, which only barely suggested the scene, made it possible to change scenes extremely quickly so that the disconnected fragments were collected as if of their own accord into a great painting of the great Revolution. Lützenkirchen as Danton emphasized above all the agitator and was really only a bubble that rises from the sea."[3] Already a major difficulty became evident in this early production: the relatively straightforward nature of Robespierre, played by Max Graumann, versus the demanding, problematic role of Danton, a many-faceted, enigmatic personality, a challenge for the best actor.

The succeeding period marked a turning point in

the reception and representation of *Danton's Death*. The German theater came under the spell of the absolute director who could completely alter the emphasis or balance of a drama and exploit it as a vehicle to promote his own ideas. On the positive side of the ledger, Büchner's play gained in popular acceptance and was recognized as a classic of the stage. On the negative side, it was often distorted to demonstrate a one-sided social view. The masses gradually came to monopolize the dramatic interest. Büchner the realist had to make way for Büchner the ecstatic expressionist.

When Max Reinhardt first staged *Danton's Death* for the Deutsche Theater on 15 December 1916, he ushered in the tradition of personalized interpretation and set a very convincing example for all subsequent productions of the drama. The private tragedy of a particular fate faded before the preponderant role of the masses, an impression which Reinhardt enhanced significantly by his suggestive use of lighting; darkness was reserved for the anonymous, amorphous crowd, while light served to distinguish the individual monumental pose. Eventually light seemed to succumb completely to darkness. To give the play structure, two large round pillars, one on either side of the stage, remained throughout the entire performance. Otherwise the sets were quite simple, partly as a result of the scarcity of materials during World War I. Whereas the right-wing press attempted to minimize the revolutionary content, the left-wing quite naturally chose to stress it. Typical of the latter is the following assessment, "Despite Büchner's disdain for terrorism, which is expressed in the personality of Robespierre and his followers as well as in the portrayal of the crowd scenes, the young poet was an enthusiastic supporter of the revolutionary cause."[4]

Danton's Death was now staged almost exclusively in the manner of Reinhardt's production. In Otto Werther's Leipzig production of February 1919, the enclosing pillars reappeared, and lighting effects amidst howling mass scenes staged by a hundred student extras culminated in the positive portrayal of the revolution on stage. Public sympathy sided with Robespierre (Friedrich Lasse), while the decadent Danton (Hans von Fielitz) was justifiably executed as an enemy of the people. Several versions followed in which directors sought to outdo even Reinhardt by exaggerating his principles.

Alfred Bernau's rendering of the play at the Deutsche Volkstheater, Vienna, in May 1921 built up the flood of revolutionary humanity to such an extent that the crowd almost completely blotted out the speeches of the protagonists. Most reviewers explained the play's new popularity in terms of its proximity to expressionistic theater and were content to classify and misconstrue Büchner as a modern social revolutionist. Both the stagings of Otto Falckenberg in the Munich Kammerspiele, September 1926, and of Gustaf Gründgens in the Hamburg Kammerspiele, January 1928, ignored the historical in favor of the monumental. The ecstatic element can be readily ascertained from Gründgens's stage direction: Lucile throws herself from a scaffold into the bayonets of approaching soldiers.

The year 1929, during which there developed considerable interest in politics and revolution by leftist and rightist groups alike, witnessed a wealth of *Danton's Death* performances. The theater was frequently

seen as an educational institution designed for the discussion of contemporary social problems. In this vein,
Josef Gielen offered his reading of the political Büchner at the Dresden Schauspielhaus in May 1929, a
purely revolutionary approach underlining the visual
and emotional aspect at the expense of the philosophical or personal scenes, which were either shortened
drastically or cut altogether. An attempt to visualize
the abstract took place at the precise moment when
Camille states, "The form of state must be a transparent garment."—A light was fixed upon the ladies
seated at the table on stage who, wearing transparent
clothes, seemed almost naked. Danton and his colleagues were depicted as animals cowering under the
shade of the guillotine while Decarli's Robespierre
won the audience's full sympathy as a folk hero.

In June 1929, in the Arkadenhof of the Vienna
Rathaus (city hall) transformed into an open-air
theater, Reinhardt staged *Danton's Death* as a mass
drama. By the skillful management of large crowds,
by special lighting, and by the intensification of visual
impressions, he created a feeling of revolutionary
enthusiasm. However, because the tragedy was presented in the framework of the Vienna Festival to
commemorate the tenth anniversary of the Austrian
federal government, Reinhardt made a conscious
effort to tone down the political note. Indeed the
Arbeiterzeitung felt that the counterrevolutionary
element was more sympathetically delineated than the
revolutionary. For instance, in the middle of St. Just's
long discourse before the National Convention, which
Gielen staged as the "proclamation of . . . communist
principles,"[5] Reinhardt had Danton laugh. Since the
people also laughed, the audience was encouraged to
judge the speech in an absurd light.

The stage set-up was also of particular interest. A wide, high platform had been constructed on one side of the Rathaus with a staircase at each end. Above this main acting area rose a three-story tower in which the intimate scenes were played. As a final grand effect, the guillotine was positioned on the top of the tower which a demagogical Danton (Paul Hartmann) and his supporters climbed in the last scene. On the whole, this experiment was well received, and despite the rain, the audience remained captivated until the end.

The last important production in 1929 opened on 1 September in the Volksbühne, Berlin, under the direction of Karl Heinz Martin. It represented the climax of the politicizing tendency. Anxious to foster a revolutionary attitude in his spectators, Martin wanted to reduce the barrier of illusion between the stage and the audience. The actors addressed all speeches directly to the audience as if it were an integral part of the Paris mob. To accommodate his scheme further, he rewrote sections of the play, added a revolutionary song at the conclusion of Robespierre's oration at the National Convention, and transformed Danton into an inhuman villain, fittingly punished for the excesses of the September massacre. In comparison, Robespierre became almost likable! Peter Lorre gave an interpretation of a cruel, satanical St. Just, which Paul Fechter called "the most interesting aspect of the whole evening."[6]

In the 1930s, literary criticism began to look at Büchner's work in a more objective manner and helped release *Danton's Death* from a revolutionary bias. A desire to comprehend the drama in the context of its own age can be detected in Otto Falckenberg's version, staged at the Munich Kammerspiele in November 1937. It underscored the monotonous and

nihilistic atmosphere of the play by a historically oriented staging. Danton (Friedrich Domin) was no
longer the degenerate counterrevolutionary who de-
serves to die, but a deeply tragic individual who recognizes the senselessness of his actions. The folk hero
Robespierre (Josef Zechell) was now exposed as a
victim of a cold idealism inimical to life.

"Having recovered from frightening the nation
over the radio, Orson Welles is now turning his attention to frightening an audience inside the Mercury
Theater. He is doing it deliberately this time in a tin-
gling revival of Georg Büchner's *Danton's Death*,
which finally opened last evening [2 November 1938].
Since Mr. Welles is an erratic genius inside the theatre,
the result is overwhelming" (Brooks Atkinson).[7]
Eleven years after Max Reinhardt and his touring
company introduced Büchner to the American stage,
Orson Welles and John Houseman offered an English
translation of *Danton's Death* to open the second season of the Mercury Theater. Reminiscent of his
German-speaking predecessor, Welles utilized lighting
to create mood. Although the masses were intentionally kept off-stage, and their presence was announced
by thunderous roars from the wings or by gigantic
shadows cast against the sets, they still tended to dom-
inate the production. Danton, played by Martin
Gabel, as "a lazy man of the world," was portrayed as
the victim of a cruel, sadistic mass monster, while
Wladimir Sokoloff, who gained some notoriety as
Reinhardt's Robespierre in a 1929 Munich production,
repeated his role as the deceptive, fanatical demagogue.
Welles acted the part of St. Just "behind a grave mask
and in a booming voice with some of the melodramatic
solemnity of 'The Shadow.' " A critic of the *Daily*

Worker deplored the absence of the people on stage and a columnist for the same paper recommended that this "distortion" of French history be withdrawn.[8] After only twenty-one performances, *Danton's Death* was discontinued, the Mercury Theater folded, and Welles devoted himself to radio programs and motion pictures.

Returning to the Continent we note an increasing drift, prescribed in part by the National Socialists' control of Germany, towards realistic interpretations of *Danton's Death*. The most obvious illustration was Gustaf Gründgens' production at the Berlin Staatliche Schauspielhaus in December 1939. The revolutionary fervor of the twenties had abated, and audiences now began to hear the intimate messages that lay hidden in the personal scenes of the play. Determined to be faithful to Büchner's pessimistic view of life and his artistic intentions, Gründgens avoided making any changes or omissions except for those dictated by the needs of the theater. This approach made greater demands upon the principal actors, who now had a central, not a peripheral function to fulfill. Rising to the challenge, Gustav Knuth achieved acclaim as one of the most sought-after Dantons in his ability to suggest all the nuances of this demanding role. A critic of the *Berliner Illustrierte Nachtausgabe* observed, "Gründgens staged the brilliant work . . . with the unpathetic matter-of-factness—with a shudder we think back to the misuses exactly ten years ago—which suits it."[9]

In the initial years of the post-Second World War era, there arose a discernible tendency to stage *Danton's Death* as a terrifying example of the release of diabolical forces or as a universally valid demonstration of how revolutionary impulses can be transformed into a reign of terror and dictatorship. Two productions which followed this trend were that of Willi Rohde in the Hessian Landestheater, Darmstadt (February 1947), and Adolf Rott in the Vienna Burgtheater (April 1947). In both versions the number of scenes, the lengthy dialogues, and the obscenities were drastically cut. In Rott's interpretation, Danton (Ewald Balser), sympathetically presented as a man of humanitarian convictions and as a victim of history, occupied the center of the stage. Subsequent stagings in 1948 displayed this same propensity and concentrated upon individual destiny. Robespierre incarnated the negative side of revolution, the danger of social collapse into bloody tyranny, whereas Danton embodied the compassionate democrat who stood for revolt as a means to achieve freedom for the people. However, a growing number of people, struck by a growing sense of insecurity following the war and influenced by the success of Jean Paul Sartre's plays on the German stage, looked to Büchner as a precursor of existentialism. At Bochum's Städtische Bühnen (September 1949) and at Düsseldorf's Schauspielhaus (March 1952), director Hans Schalla singled out Büchner's deterministic concept of life and emphasized man's surrender to incomprehensible historical forces. Schalla made extensive use of what is now called in German an "iron set": three high, bare walls with a balcony formed out of iron bars and plates. The wide panoramas of the twenties were reduced to the confining single cold metallic décor of an intimate theater with doors which would open of their own accord to reveal only darkness within. In the last scene, three women, knitting red socks upon the iron balcony, represented the indifference and lack of feeling of history for its unfortunate sufferers. Lucile's arrest occasioned only a brief pause in their knitting. Several interpretations generally followed this pattern, stressing, in the words of Georg Hensel, *"Danton's Death* as a dream of human existence under the control of history, a tragedy of the distress of existence."[10] Danton personified the philosophy of the void in Oskar Wälterlin's intimate staging for the Zürich Schauspielhaus, September 1952, or in Gustav Rudolf Sellner's version for the Hessian Landestheater, September 1957. This same depressing atmosphere can be discovered in still another production by Gründgens for the Hamburg Deutsche Schauspielhaus in January 1958.

Gradually the effects of the "economic miracle" in West Germany began to mitigate this preoccupation with the deterministic outlook. A more concrete scare superseded the general fear of existence: the totalitarian system of the Eastern Block seemed to offer a serious threat to classical liberalism with its belief in the supremacy of the individual. By drawing some rather explicit parallels between the French Revolution and the Communist Revolution of 1917, Robespierre could easily be cast in the role of a communist party chief and Danton as his victim. A 1951 staging directed by Hans Schweikart in the Munich Kammerspiele saw Danton turn his back to the court and speak directly in his defense to the spectators. At the same time, loudspeakers boomed out the accusations leveled at the revolutionary leader from behind the audience, a symbolic representation of the anonymous, machine-like omnipresence and omnipotence of the authoritarian state. This same political message can be detected in Gillis van Rappard's 1952 staging for the

Lippische Landestheater, Detmold, in which the guillotine blade fell five times to the hysterical cries of the
masses. "The democracy of the old Jacobins and the
People's Democracy of our neighbors [East Ger-
many] offer a very surprising parallel," commented
Walter Falke who reviewed the play.[11]

Erwin Piscator returned to Germany in 1952 to
stage *Danton's Death* for the Marburg Schauspiel and
the Stadttheater at Giessen. The set designer Erhardt
Klonck built a podium in the middle of the theater
with a walkway connecting it to the proscenium. An
additional bridge led from the stage to a guillotine
standing at the back. In keeping with his documentary
style, Piscator presented the drama as a vivid recreation of the historic events in Paris. Two gauze walls
served as a screen against which pictures of the real
protagonists, death lists, records, etc., were projected
to give the production an aura of authenticity. In all,
forty-two slides (including one of Georg Büchner at
the conclusion) introduced and accompanied the action, much of which took place in the middle of the
audience. Extras even sat amongst the spectators, yell-
ing their approval or disapproval of the speeches. In
1956 Piscator repeated the experiment for the Schillertheater, Berlin, an exciting performance but one with
a decidedly didactic intent. H. Zehder, writing for *Die
Welt*, summarized aptly: "For the masses Piscator
erected the rotating monster of his staircase, the structure of ascent, crowned with the guillotine above the
haunts of the bourgeoisie. The human side, the so-
called human freedom of the individual as a democratic factor, got the short end of the stick. The
human, the private sphere, became secondary in view
of the social change that was being fulfilled."[12]

In perhaps the most famous non-German speaking production of *Danton's Death*, Jean Vilar contributed significantly to the recognition of Büchner's international appeal and "modernity." In this now celebrated version performed by the Théâtre National Populaire, Daniel Ivernel played the part of Danton.

FRENCH EMBASSY, OTTAWA, CANADA

Jean Vilar had to overcome considerable opposition before his successful 1952 Paris première of *Danton's Death*, translated into French by Arthur Adamov. Several critics objected that Vilar's Théâtre National Populaire was patronizing too many foreign authors in an institution supported by state money. To convince his detractors of the suitability of Büchner's drama, he held an evening of readings in a small theater on the left bank and won over his critics. Vilar opted to produce *Danton's Death* against a black background on an almost empty stage. All required props were carried on and off the set by costumed stage hands or the actors themselves. Depth, expanse, and other visual effects were suggested through lighting techniques while color was provided by the predominantly red, white, and blue costumes of the performers. Since Vilar created "a sequence of frescolike pictures from the French Revolution,"[13] some reviewers expressed the opinion that his approach was simply "too historical."

The 1950s also witnessed an important British interpretation of Büchner's play. A new organization called the Fifty Nine Theatre Company produced a *Danton's Death* in the Lyric Theater, Hammersmith, January 1959, which the critic of *The Times* referred to as a "collector's piece, though the power of this dramatist has been increasingly recognized in Europe and America."[14] This interpretation chose to concentrate upon the personal dilemma of the main protagonists. "Mr. Patrick Wymark [Danton] gives us both the fine eloquent public side of the hero and the misgivings which spring so readily from the other side of his nature. He is both in public and in private something of a poseur, but Mr. Wymark well establishes the vein of honesty which runs through both the demagogue and the introspect." Harold Lang proved somewhat deficient in the role of Robespierre, but Patrick McGoohan as St. Just was "completely effective." The typical problems which have beset directors since the 1902 première again made their presence felt: the necessity of rapid scene changes, the lack of a sufficiently large and flexible cast, and the need for good actors even in small parts. *Danton's Death* has always put the theatrical skill and resources of a company to the test and has contributed to the demise of more than one.

Danton's Death, officially designated as "a wonderful work—unfortunately unperformable,"[15] had to wait until July 1962 for its debut in the German Democratic Republic (East Germany). Marxist literary critics preferred to see in Büchner the social revolutionary while ignoring his repudiation of revolution in his first play. How then was it possible to reconcile this attitude with an East German production? "The first German poet who knew that history often can only give birth to something new under pain, the first who was not frightened to see [history] twisting and turning in revolutionary labor pains was called Georg Büchner," wrote an anonymous East German critic. The national prize winner Kuba completely revised the drama to fashion "a beautiful example of a fruitful, biased approach" in a manner reminiscent of the politically oriented versions of the twenties. Not limiting himself merely to shortening scenes and combining others, a now accepted practice, Kuba proceeded to rewrite the whole tragedy so that Danton became a "regenerate, traitor, and bourgeois" who deserved to be destroyed by the revolution. Also, in accordance with another established tradition, the production alluded to a contemporary political situation: the justification and glorification of Robespierre could easily be construed as a defense of Stalin (Kuba was the author of a Stalin cantata!) in response to Khrushchev's destalinization policy first announced at the Twentieth Party Congress in 1956.

In February 1963 Hans Schalla once again directed

Danton's Death, this time for the city of Essen, in which he again underlined the deterministic feeling for life so characteristic of many passages in Büchner's correspondence. Reviewing this production, Willy Haas of *Die Welt* commented, "It is the most consistent poetic document of a consistent representative of materialism, the only real one which Germany has produced and who went even further than Bertholt Brecht."[16] Schalla's Danton, played to perfection by Herbert Suschka, can no longer act, indeed refuses to act, while explaining the grounds for his indolence in one endless monologue, "the backbone of the drama." Interestingly, Robespierre's opposition party, also juxtaposed with Stalinism was seen here in an unsympathetic, terrifying light, while St. Just morally justifies the extermination of thousands including the innocent in the interest of a revolutionary ideal.

"Herbert Blau and Jules Irving, the new artistic directors of the Lincoln Center Repertory Theater, have associated President Johnson with Robespierre, Mao Tse-tung, Fidel Castro, and Prime Minister Henrik F. Verwoerd of South Africa in an article on *Danton's Death*, a nineteenth-century drama of the French Revolution attacking dictatorship," wrote Milton Esterow.[17] The article further revealed that on the American continent as well directors persisted in interpreting Büchner within their own social context. The atrocities of the French Revolution became synonymous with Vietnam and "releasing napalm over the jungle." Some even saw shades of Senator Goldwater in Robert Symond's Robespierre.

Unfortunately, this politicized New York production, a questionable *succès de scandale*, was designed to mark the opening of the new Vivian Beaumont

Theater in the Lincoln Center for the Performing Arts. Singled out for praise were the portrayal of St. Just by the black actor R. L. Browne, Jo Mielziner's sets, "which use great thrusting lines to achieve perspective in depth and which evoke the streets and gardens of the surging city,"[18] and the final prison scene where "[all] that is needed is the play of light as if filtered through barred windows, capable actors, and the fierce, probing words of a poet."[19] But the critics of both the New York *Times* and the London *Times* unanimously deplored the poor acting and the lack of a unifying message. "What is worse is that as a whole, it says nothing to us. People and events are simply seen on the stage; some are interesting and some are not, but the play itself conveys no meaning and no excitement."[20]

Danton proved to be too demanding for Alan Bergmann, who resorted to heroic poses and succeeded in suggesting only one side of a complex personality. In his review, entitled "Büchner Too Much for New York Company," the London *Times* correspondent noted quite perceptively, "This early nineteenth-century tragedy about Danton's last struggle against Robespierre must surely be one of the hardest great plays to stage successfully, even in the best of circumstances."[21]

Fernando Arrabal once remarked, "We are living under the dictatorship of directors. What people today call theater is a rape committed against the text of the authors."[22] Judging from the storm of criticism, largely negative, which Hans Neuenfels's two similar productions of *Danton's Death* (October 1969, Heidelberg, and October 1975, Bochum) gave rise to, one would have to lend some credence to Arrabal's observation. In an attempt to arrive at a collective and systematized dramatic style, two months of "theater work"[23] preceded the Heidelberg première, during which an experimental formula was devised to break through the traditional theatrical prejudices and to rescue Büchner "from the peace of the grave of the classical authors."[24]

As the program explained it: "We have removed the external train of action from the play; we have put in its place concepts, argumentation, provocation, identification, exhibition. The dramatic happening was therefore turned into a play of permanent discussion, into scraps of conversation after the Revolution."[25] As soon as Neuenfels had read over a loudspeaker Büchner's letter that begins, "If anything is to help in our times, then it's force," the lights revealed an immense white shroud draped over the whole stage upon which the actors, remaining constantly on the set and arranging themselves in picturesque poses, played their parts without a scene change and with a bare minimum of props in a record one and a half hours. Because of the almost exclusive emphasis upon the word seconded by pantomime, many novel techniques were attempted.

Most of the controversy centered around Neuenfels use of montage whereby passages from Büchner, Proust, Mörike, Kafka and Lautréamont were incorporated into the dialogue. While Danton repeated the wording of the introductory Büchner letter before Robespierre, Camille spoke some lines which normally appear much later in the drama, and as long as Danton and Julie engaged in their private dialogue of the first scene, Lucile, facing the audience, recited a famous Proust passage dealing with memory. A con-

troversial example of living theater which was at-
tacked by a radical student group even before the first
performance, it led to completely contradictory reactions. On the one hand we read, "[On stage] neither a
person, nor a situation, nor even a 'permanent discussion' can be developed. . . . Robespierre makes his
speeches as if they consisted of figures of speech in
which he himself doesn't believe" (Georg Hensel).[26]

But Gert Kalow (*Frankfurter Allgemeine Zeitung*)
wrote, "Above all, the predominance of language in
Büchner is correct, as it is here maintained and for-
tunately also realized. . . . First to be mentioned is
Gottfried John (Robespierre) who knew how to fas-
cinate with scanty means."[27] The Bochum version,
equally disquieting, opened with Julie's visiting her
husband in a brothel and ended with Robespierre's
inviting the unhappy Lucile to join him for a drink in
a local café. Although these acts of textual violence are
consistently justified by directors in terms of desirable
modernization, one must seriously ask oneself if such
flippant changes, as Julie's sending Marion to the imprisoned Danton with a kiss, do justice to a drama that
has been known to stand on its own merit.

Büchner's first tragedy would seem to be a frequent
choice as a work to inaugurate a theater, a bold but
often fatal decision as already experienced by Blau and
Irving in New York. In January 1970, approximately
six hundred policemen, some on horseback, others
with guard dogs, formed a protective corridor down
which the guests invited to the opening of the Düsseldorf Schauspielhaus walked to the accompaniment
of insults and slogans shouted by angry demonstrators
objecting to the exclusion of the general public. Need-
less to say, the external protest detracted considerably

in its sensationalism from the internal performance directed by Karl-Heinz Stroux, who chose to stress the nihilistic and fatalistic elements by concentrating more upon the individual conflicts than the crowd scenes.

Wilfred Minks designed an hermetic set which continually displayed all necessary props scattered about a synchronized acting area. Special visual effects were achieved by constructing several stage levels that could all be viewed at the same time. The prison was located below the stage. Above it on another level a soldier stood on guard, and finally a staircase rose to the Tribunal where St. Just (Wolfgang Reinbacher) at the lectern, supported by Robespierre (Hans Caninenberg), created an overwhelming theatrical effect. Wolfgang Reichmann's Danton allowed audiences to glimpse the man of action behind his lethargy, a portrayal deemed especially noteworthy in the readings of the play's introspective, reflective passages. But once again was heard a familiar criticism leveled at many productions of this complex, cumbersome masterpiece—the lack of a unifying principle of interpretation. In the assessment of Hans Schwab-Felisch, "Even chaos on stage demands form."[28]

In 1971 the National Theater in London sought to stage the play, under the direction of Jonathan Miller, around the conflicting personalities and views of Danton and Robespierre seen as victims of historical forces beyond their control. Availing himself of the puppet image from Danton's Death and aided by Patrick Robertson's sets, Miller sketched a mechanical view of life. At the start, the ominous sight of a series of boxes containing decapitated models in costume confronted the audience. Towards the end of the performance,

Danton and his supporters returned to their respective boxes like marionettes who had fulfilled their function. Christopher Plummer gave a monumental portrayal of Danton, and Charles Kay admirably suggested the tormented private soul of the perverted idealist Robespierre. "All [the actors] contributed to a production which, though it lacks factitious excitement, gets straight to the essence of Büchner" (Michael Billington).[29]

The same year saw an additional rendering of *Danton's Death* in Glasgow, Scotland, which furnished a very marked contrast to the London version. "Two delicate, satin-clad figures sit frozen at a downstage card-table, flanked by the music stands of an invisible orchestra. But for an occasional blink, they might be waxworks, emblems of a potential world bounded by prettiness and pleasure. Then the Boucher-like tableau dissolves. White curtains are ripped down revealing a crazy labyrinth of tricolour scaffoldings and five blood-red fire escapes; and the rococo dolls turn aghast, the cards flutter from their hands, as a revolutionary crowd surges forward drowning the court orchestra with choruses of 'Ça ira.' Such is the opening of Keith Hack's production of *Danton's Death* at the Glasgow Citizens' Theatre" (Irving Wardle).[30]

Whereas the National Theater interpretation was coldly executed in a more traditional vein, this production thrived on daring innovations including the scenery, designed by Philip Prowse, who once stated, "all my sets are death traps."[31] Ian McDianmid as St. Just declaimed his long speech from the top of the décor before a fifteen-foot drop; and while Lucile acted out her final desperate suicidal gesture, the figure of Robespierre could be seen above the stage, meticulously working at his desk. It was an extremely energetic, enthusiastic performance, which made severe demands on the bodies and the voices of a basically young eighteen-member company.

Toward the beginning of December 1971, the old Stockholm Parliament Building was metamorphosed into the site of a revolutionary happening as the Swedish singer Monica Nielson, standing at a balcony window on the second floor, sung the famous revolutionary song "Ça ira" over a loudspeaker. At the side of the building stood the foreboding framework of the guillotine. As soon as the doors were thrown open and the public surged into this classically designed edifice, soldiers with fixed bayonets and screaming men and women mingled with the crowd and the first street scene from *Danton's Death* began to unfold. Innovative thinking on the part of Michael Meschke, the director of a Swedish puppet theater, resulted in one of the most intriguing experimental stagings of Büchner's tragedy.

Although its Swedish première had taken place three years ago in Göteborg, this second production in the rented Parliament Building proved unforgettable and unique, an example of total theater, since the audience had no other alternative but to become actively involved. "[The] significance of the house played the preponderant role, its function as a political stage which here was directly taken over."[32] Following the call of Robespierre, the masses, including the paying patrons, headed for the Jacobin Club, the parliamentary assembly room where most of the remaining scenes took place. Meschke exploited theatrically every nook and cranny of the old structure. For those intimate, moving moments, one of the several niches of the large assembly room was suddenly illuminated.

The production achieved a climax with the meeting of the National Convention where St. Just and Robes-pierre arouse the mob to a vociferous condemnation of the Dantonists. All those present seemed to rise in a single body, an impression reinforced by actors stra-tegically located in the balcony or the aisles. Danton's defense before the Revolutionary Tribunal was rele-gated to a high-walled corridor where the prisoners were rolled in upon a large table on casters. For the concluding prison sequence, the onlooker was obliged to move again, this time to a large staircase, the land-ing of which represented the conciergerie. Finally, soldiers conducted the condemned down the stairs to the courtyard and the guillotine, visible through a glass door.

While the masses descended the staircase, hungry for blood, and a drum roll announced the execution, Julie spread Danton's coat on the edge of the landing, kneeled upon it, took poison, and collapsed, almost unnoticed by the others. Once more the singer came into view at the balcony to sing "Ça ira." "[Meschke's] staging of *Danton's Death* in the old Parliament Building is a resounding success in Stockholm and is finding a predominantly young audience. [His] stag-ing intends to deglorify revolution as an end in itself and to show how people fail, break down when they are confronted with power. He deals with the gener-ally valid human attitude in a revolutionary situation," wrote Elke Lehmann-Brauns.[33] That the success of this experiment depended to a large degree upon the setting was amply and painfully demonstrated by its rather cool critical reception at the Berlin Festival in

In this controversial *vocal* production of *Danton's Death*, director Jürgen Flimm opted to emphasize the fate of the individual as represented by both Danton and Robespierre. The photograph depicts Harold Kuhlmann as Lacroix, Hans-Michael Rehberg as Danton, Dietmar Mues as Hérault-Séchelles, and Heinz Gerhard Lück as Philippeau.

HELGA KNEIDL, HAMBURG

October 1972. "The University of Fine Arts is not a parliament building; not even as an edifice does it meet the demands of historical authenticity since it was constructed in 1902 in a kind of neo-baroque style," wrote Günter Grack.[34]

In November 1976 the Deutsche Schauspielhaus, Hamburg, presented a literally ear-splitting interpretation directed by Jürgen Flimm. Keeping close to Büchner's text, which since the days of Reinhardt has often been arbitrarily abused, Flimm accented the personal dilemma of man caught up in an unfathomable world order governed by the "horrible fatalism of history." As Rolf Michaelis, writing for *Die Zeit*, observed, "Here Büchner is taken seriously and at his word. We hear what we otherwise only read, what other performances mostly only allude to; i.e., that in the play, the faster the characters are driven to the scaffold, the more they scream. . . ."[35] At every opportunity, and *Danton's Death* provides several, actors shrieked at the top of their lungs in a veritable "orgy of screams" which succeeded in getting on the nerves of the audience. To reinforce the private note, even the political theme was centered in the romantic Danton (Hans-Michael Rehberg) and the pragmatic Robespierre (Herbert Mensching), both of whom were viewed as equally justified and hence equally tragic. With this concentration upon the conflict between counterrevolution dictated by human compassion and revolution conducted under the sign of terror, Michaelis emphasized the "surprising actuality" of the production vis-à-vis the contemporary political debate. Interestingly, directors and critics continue to regard *Danton's Death* in the light of their own political or existential plight, but the pendulum has swung completely away from the predominance of the masses in productions from the 1920s to the individual dimension of the hero or antihero caught in the absurd web of life.

4. *LEONCE AND LENA*

Leonce, the prince of Popo (a German colloquial expression for buttocks), is a victim of that *mal du siècle* called boredom. The efforts of Valerio, the royal fool and master of pun, prove ineffective in dispersing the general mood of oppressive melancholy and even contribute to an impression of inescapable monotony. Nothing can be expected from King Peter, a dim-witted monarch who spends all his time and effort constructing and living according to a meaningless philosophical system. Rosetta, formerly a royal favorite of Leonce's, seeks to rekindle the flame of passion in the prince, but love has become one in a long series of dissatisfying, dull experiences, a routine which one follows out of sheer habit. Since this form of entertainment does not offer the prospect of something new, Rosetta is dismissed as a mere flirtation. The President appears before Leonce to announce the expected arrival of Princess Lena of Pipi (a popular expression for urine) to whom by royal decree the prince has been betrothed. Never having set eyes upon her, Leonce decides to avoid this state marriage by fleeing toward the south. His escape is juxtaposed with a scene in which Lena in the company of her governess is trying to flee from a similar predicament, that of being forced to accept a husband whom she does not love.

The second act depicts the fateful union of the young lovers. Without being aware of their respective identities, they meet by chance in the proximity of a country tavern and are irresistibly drawn towards one another. The confrontation achieves its climax with a kiss in the idyllic setting of a moonlit garden. Feeling that his whole being was centered in that moment, Leonce is only prevented from casting himself into the river by the intervention of Valerio. Irony reduces an apparent suicide attempt to a mere heroic pose: "Hey, you've just deprived me of the most beautiful suicide."

The third and final act returns us to the Kingdom of Popo where preparations for the wedding are under way. The schoolmaster is lining up the peasants along the royal route, instructing them in, or coercing them into proper behavior. "Don't scratch behind your ears and don't blow your nose as long as the noble couple drives by." King Peter's whole philosophical system is thrown out of joint when he learns from the President and the Master of Ceremonies that the bride and groom have absconded, but at the last minute, Leonce and Lena, accompanied by their confidants, appear in masks and are introduced to the court by Valerio as mechanical puppets. It is decided to go through with the marriage in proxy so that King Peter may rejoice as planned. Once the ceremony has been performed, the masks are removed and the true identities revealed in a stereotypical operatic conclusion.

LEONCE: I've been deceived!
LENA: I've been deceived!
LEONCE: O chance!
LENA: O providence!

Having decided to devote himself exclusively to thinking, King Peter abdicates in favor of his son, who
proposes a new community based on laziness, pleasure,
and physical comfort under the state leadership of
Valerio.

"Look here, first of all I have to spit on this stone
here three hundred and sixty-five times in succession."
Our first encounter with the central figure of this
comedy reveals him as stricken with the incurable and
often fatal disease of the modern age, ennui. The
young prince views spitting upon a stone or counting
grains of sand as equally significant as learning to rule
his country. Even great metaphysical issues such as the
existence of God, when juxtaposed with the ludicrous
pastime of Leonce, become banal. All human aspirations
and achievements share the same absurd fate. Cursed
with this awareness, the bored young man craves a
flight into a surrealistic realm. "O, happy the man who
could see himself once upon his head!" The realization
of something new and physically impossible, a breaking out from the depressing normality of daily existence would perhaps save him. Rhetorical self-interro-
gation, "Am I a loafer? Don't I have anything to do
now?" implies a desire to disregard this pose and discover some different and meaningful activity. But
after boredom follows melancholy, the state of mind
of Danton or the Captain in *Woyzeck*. "The fact that
for three weeks now the clouds have been moving
from west to east makes me very melancholy." An
existential sadness grounded in the very nature of life

itself, it asks why man is refused the means to surpass the ineluctable laws of cause and effect or why he is incapable of transcending the usual or the normal.

"Just look how people do everything out of boredom! They study out of boredom, they pray out of boredom, they fall in love, marry, and reproduce out of boredom, and finally die out of boredom, and—and that's the humor of it—they do it all with the most serious faces without noticing why and think only God knows what." Just as Danton achieves the insight that all men are "epicureans," in like manner Leonce classifies all men as "loafers." Sainthood, heroics, and even paternity are mere stances, necessitated by the need to avoid recognition of the true human condition. "Why must I of all people know it? Why can't I give myself airs and put a tailcoat on the poor puppet and stick an umbrella in its hand so that it may become very honest and very useful and very moral?" Once one has arrived at this discernment, one can no longer deceive oneself and willingly accept the puppet role of society—fulfilling what is normally expected of the ideal citizen. Since disillusionment destroys the relevance of middle-class virtues, the recipient of this fateful knowledge can only resent those who enjoy the bliss of ignorance. "The man who just left me, I envied him, I would have liked to thrash him out of envy. O, happy the man who for once could be someone else!"

One of the most perceptive as well as truly entertaining characters in this comedy is Valerio, whose prototype may be found in the figure of the Shakespearian fool or the Harlequin of commedia dell'arte. Too pragmatic to be deceived by appearances, he delights in satirizing the current "romantic sentiments" by a reductio ad absurdum. "Ah, my Lord, what a feeling I have for nature! The grass grows so beautifully that one would like to be an ox in order to be able to eat it and then a human being again in order to eat the ox who had eaten such grass."

Leonce recognizes in his amusing companion a kindred spirit who thinks too much and who must resort to tomfoolery to dispel a deep-seated dissatisfaction with himself. "Unhappy man, you [Valerio] also seem to be afflicted with ideals." Since Valerio refuses to accept the physical limitations of man according to natural law—"It's a pity! One can't jump down from a church steeple without breaking one's neck"—a sense of frustration would threaten to overwhelm him if he were not astute enough to play the fool. Neither truth which cripples nor reason which registers man's wretchedness offers any real salvation, whereas folly enables the individual to create a world of pleasant and comfortable illusions. Verbal wit and all forms of humor devised by Valerio to induce laughter are basically a defense mechanism to cover up life's tragic implications.

In the final scene of the play, Valerio makes an important long speech which revolves around one of Büchner's favorite images, that of the puppet. The more down-to-earth side of the jester's personality accounts for his decidedly materialistic behavior, which breaks through the comical surface level. His confession—"I don't know anything at all about what I am saying, indeed I also don't even know that I don't know it so that it is highly probable that they only let me speak this way and that it is really nothing but cylinders and windpipes which say everything. . . . Nothing but art and mechanism, nothing but pasteboard and watch springs!"—should not be disregarded as linguistic nonsense, for it provides a clear indication of the mechanics of human life.

Referring to the masked Leonce and Lena, Valerio further observes, "These persons are so perfectly constructed that one can't distinguish them at all from other human beings. If one didn't know that they're only pasteboard, one could readily make them into members of the human race." This statement directly parallels the speeches of the barker in *Woyzeck*. In the latter play, man, compared to a horse, is debased to a stage equal to, if not lower than, that of the beast. Resorting to the same method in *Leonce and Lena*, Büchner gives a concrete demonstration of how man, a supposedly free agent, differs in no significant way from the puppet.

These marionette-like figures are noble since they speak standard German and ethical because they act in accordance with the conventions of the times. "They also have a good digestive system, which proves that they have a good conscience." Morality, in addition to being an expression of social convention, has a positivistic explanation. A good constitution points to a good conscience, a luxury which can be afforded only by those wealthy enough to keep their stomachs filled. Even love comes under the mechanical rule of cause and effect as Valerio depicts a typical courtship.

Büchner's correspondence discloses a distrust of philosophy and its language, his rejection of its often meaningless abstract terminology, and his preference for a realistic, common-sense approach rather than the purely speculative. King Peter, an adherent of idealistic philosophy, becomes the target of Büchner's highly effective satire. Nothing can destroy an individual or a notion more quickly or completely than ridicule. A fool who runs about on stage half-naked, maintaining that he must think for his subjects, calls into question the very system he expounds.

The Captain of *Woyzeck* and the King are two of the same kind. The latter's "In itself is in itself" calls to mind the Captain's imbecile utterance, "Morality, that's when one is moral." Although Peter refers to his clothing as "attributes, modifications, deceits, and accidents," i.e., as not being crucial to his substance or real self, the ludicrous figure of a naked mentally deficient monarch emphasizes the well-known platitude that clothes do indeed make the man. Philosophical concepts such as free will and morality are juxtaposed with the utter confusion of the *lever* (the morning dressing of a monarch). In fact, Peter's "whole system is ruined" simply because "the snuff box isn't in the right pocket." The ultimate ironical situation arises when the ruler, who purports to think for his subjects, discovers the purpose of a knot tied in his handkerchief: "I wanted to remind myself of my people." A caricature of a king who forgets his people can be explained by Büchner's vehement hatred for the aristocracy. In addition to this implied social-revolutionary note, Peter, despite his royal pretensions, is exposed as a normal or, better stated, subnormal human being. As in *The Hessian Messenger*, Büchner reduces a head of state to the common human denominator of his nakedness.

Both King Peter and the Captain tend to be long-winded and subject to periods of melancholy based on a deep-seated fear: "When I [Peter] speak so loudly, then I don't know who it really is, I or someone else. That frightens me . . . I am I," or on some intangible psychological course: "It terrifies me [Captain] when I think that the world revolves in one day!" Büchner dramatically presents two almost retarded individuals whose peace of mind is seriously threatened by anything that surpasses their deficient minds and who take refuge in confusion, putting the blame on someone actually superior in intelligence. In both characterizations, the question of identity and the fear of its loss stress an awareness of personal insignificance.

Valerio continues the satire on the ruling class when he informs Leonce, "you are to become king. That's a fun affair." Royal duties are defined as spending the day in pleasure-seeking, forcing the people to remove their hats in subservience, and compelling subjects to become soldiers or court servants "so that everything becomes quite natural." This ironical comment serves to underline the complete opposite, the constrained, artificial necessity of keeping up regal appearances. Through the court jester, Büchner calls into question the whole concept of kingship, denouncing it as a repressive, unjust, purposeless institution. While the President in the concluding scene of the play attempts to placate the King with his meaningless chatter, he inadvertently utters a truth which the author of *The Hessian Messenger* heartily endorses. "A royal word is a thing—a thing—which is nothing."

"[The people] are managing so well in their suffering that for some time now they have been depending upon one another. Resolutely they pour alcohol into one another; otherwise it would be impossible for them to be able to hold out so long in this heat." The ruler chooses to ignore completely and even to turn to his advantage the misfortunes of his subjects: "Recognize what they are doing for you: they have positioned you in such a manner that the wind from the kitchen goes over you, and for once in your life you are smelling a roast." Although the presence of the peasants, a traditional source of comedy, is fully exploited as a vehicle for humor (they are depicted as typical country bumpkins, uncultivated and ignorant), still in *Leonce and Lena* Büchner, the lover of the people, cannot deny his concern for their material welfare.

The comedy concerns itself primarily with the various attempts on the part of Leonce to escape from the clutches of boredom. The first avenue explored is that of entertainment, the desire to submerge the ever-alert mind in the sensuality of wine, woman, and song. The vivacious and coquettish Rosetta appears at one time to have met the prince's demand for amusement and to have helped him forget temporarily his human limitations. Now his love for her is designated both as a form of work and as a further source of boredom, sleep, and oblivion. Although Rosetta's wit and levity enable her to dismiss Leonce's theatrics as self-satisfying poses, the final impression with which she leaves the audience is one of isolation.

> I am a poor orphan.
> I'm afraid all alone,
> Ah, dear sorrow.
> Won't you come home with me?

A lost soul in a hostile world, she is obsessed above all by the fear of being cut off from human contact, the tragic situation of Danton, Robespierre, or the child in the black fairy tale of *Woyzeck*. Songs might be expected to emphasize the lightness and joy of a comedy, but in this one they accentuate the pessimism underlying the humor.

Other forms of evasion are considered, such as an escape into the self, the return to nature, or even death, but no sooner are they proposed than they are rejected as unsatisfactory. One of the last scenes of the first act offers an additional catalogue of various means to avoid cognition of the human condition. "Ah, science, science! Let's become scholars! A priori? or a posteriori?" This particular distraction provides Büchner with ample opportunity to satirize the academic community. "A priori, that one has to learn from my dear father." Hero worship or the pursuit of glory through military powers, typical romantic motifs as exemplified in the early Heine's admiration for Napoleon, are decried by Leonce as empty values. "But heroism becomes terribly frayed and gets hospital fever and can't exist without lieutenants and recruits. Get lost with your Alexander and Napoleon romanticism!" Romantic overtones are stripped away disclosing the ugly, repulsive side of war. The much heralded general is dwarfed and rendered insignificant before the greater mass of soldiers who decide the dice roll of history. Even within the limitations of the comedy, Büchner the realist cannot refrain from destroying the heartwarming illusions with which man surrounds his endeavors.

After rejecting the genius cult of the storm-and-stress movement and practical idealism as espoused by the German middle class, Leonce suggests the final evasive tactic, a flight into the south. "Don't you feel the wind blowing from the south? We'll go to Italy." A luxurious paradise, it must be felt, seen and heard. Blue skies, golden-sunny earth, marble columns and bodies all combine their sensual powers to put the intellect to sleep. The slumbering Pan, the memory of a wild orgiastic age, statues which dream of the old magician Virgil, or the passion and violence of the tarantella reveal Leonce's predilection for free if not violent expression of the vital instincts. This speech contains many typical romantic themes such as the yearning for the south or the desire to assume the role of a "Lazzaroni," a Neapolitan good-for-nothing, while the emphasis placed upon the sensual, orgiastic elements, all of which are expressed with an underlying tone of death, anticipates the Eros-Thanatos dichotomy and ambiguity of the second act.

Whereas death is merely implied in Leonce's vision of Italy, it is more explicitly expressed in our introduction to the heroine of the comedy. "Look, I wish the lawn would grow over me like that and the bees would hum along above me; look, now I'm dressed and have rosemary in my hair. Isn't there an old song: 'In the graveyard I want to lie/Like a wee child in the cradle.' "? Death and nature, closely related in Lena's speech, form part of a natural cycle based on life (birth) and decay (graveyard). This staging was obviously inspired by a similar episode in *Hamlet*, specifically Ophelia's madness during which, overcome by suffering occasioned by unrequited love and the death of her father, she discusses the symbolic value of flowers and thus foretells her return to the elements by her suicidal drowning.[1] This strange literary association of a comic with a tragic heroine is yet another indication of the tragic basis of *Leonce and Lena*. It is not a question of unrequited love, the predicament faced by Ophelia, but rather of denied love. Compelled by political expediency to marry someone she has never met, Lena has chosen flight rather than a loveless union.

Generally in Büchner's works, women have a marked tendency towards nonintellectualism. Each is primarily aware of herself as one who loves and wants to be loved in return, and solely when this basic drive is thwarted does she become a tragic figure. Lena more or less fits into this mold, but she raises the crucial issue of human suffering on a universal level. "My God, my God, is it then true that we must redeem ourselves through our pain? Is it then true that the world is a crucified savior, the sun its crown of thorns, and the stars the nails and spears in his feet and thighs?" According to one Christian tradition, we have to attain our own salvation by merit of the suffering we undergo in life, the same answer Büchner is said to have arrived at upon his deathbed. "We don't have too much pain, we have too little of it, for through pain we go to God!" While the whole world becomes the crucified one, an underlying, emotional question asks why this must be the case. The theme of human affliction is so central to Büchner's view of life that it even becomes an integral part of his only comedy. The solution offered here, since it is formulated as a query and no answer is offered, suggests the inadmissibility of the explanation.

The first act of *Leonce and Lena* has served primarily to acquaint the audience with the intellectual disposition or malady of the hero and to indicate several futile attempts to escape from the conscious realization of the human condition. This long exposition contributes meaningfully to the dramatic confrontation of the two similarly inclined lovers, the woman being introduced only at the end of the act.

While the Governess, a stock figure of the traditional romance, acts her part well, thoroughly enjoying the romantic, sentimental element, Lena, except for one emotional outburst of enthusiasm: "Oh [the world] is beautiful and so wide, so endlessly wide!" seems to be conscious of a tragic undercurrent. The Governess who expects to find monasteries, hermits, or shepherds, who dreams of "a wandering prince," and who delights in drawing parallels between her actual situation and the plots of popular novels, lives in an illusionary realm. "It's a renunciation. It's like the flight of Saint Ottilia." Her romantic images, fostered by books, are a poor substitute for a cold reckoning with reality.

Lena aptly observes: "We have dreamed of everything quite differently with our books behind the wall of our garden amongst our myrtle and oleander bushes." Her confidante's remark about "a wandering prince," in addition to being a humorous example of dramatic irony since Leonce has just left the stage, underscores the fairy-tale aura and the subsequent contrived impression with which the comedy leaves the audience. A happy ending will be possible only because this is a fairy tale. Büchner leaves the impression, just as Molière does with the concocted deus-ex-machina conclusion of his *Tartuffe*, that life in reality is just not like this.

The stage is set for the first meeting conducted under the sign of Thanatos. "The ticking of the death clock in our breasts is slow and every drop of blood measures its time and our life is a creeping fever." Lena continues the metaphors initiated by Leonce, an exchange which dramatically suggests two kindred spirits meant for each other. Captivated by her voice,

Leonce intuits a secret rapport. "[But] I have under-stood [this voice]. It rests upon me like the spirit when it hovered above the waters before there was light. What ferment in the depth, what genesis in me, how the voice pours through space!"

Before this encounter, Leonce was part of the empty darkness prior to the creation of life. Like the formless, desolate world, he knew only the void, only the night and despair of delving into himself. Lena's voice is analogous to that of God, "Let there be light." Just as the divine decree created light and life, Lena gives Leonce the hope of a new, meaningful existence, a possibility of achieving communication through true love, the only solution other than death itself now open to the disheartened prince.

Leonce and Lena has consciously been raised by Büchner to the level of the unreal, the magical, the implication being that the truly happy, contented man can only exist in a world of childlike illusion. Happi-ness and reality are incompatible. The fairy tale is the ultimate escape, and love the means to this end. It corresponds to the inborn wish in man to escape to paradise, to lose his self-consciousness, which distin-guishes him from the other animals, and to become one and live in perfect harmony with the natural world, a unity destroyed by man's objective distance from himself. The desire to retreat to Eden, and the awareness of the self as a being who must die, form the psychological motivation behind the verbal and physical confrontation between Leonce and Lena.

The setting of the final scenes of the second act: the garden suggestive of the innocence and purity of paradise, the moon-lit night with the ambivalence of love and death, prepares the audience for the climactic high point of the drama. Representative of an objective, noninvolved point of view, Valerio commences with a satire on the romantic vision of nature, a further example of Büchner's preference for unadorned reality. "Nature is a beautiful thing, but she would be even more beautiful if there were no gnats, if her beds were somewhat cleaner, and if the death-watch beetles didn't peck away like that in the walls."

The physical world with its gnats and beetles reminds us that all organisms, including man, are subject to nature's cycle of life and death. "Inside men snore and outside frogs croak, inside the house crickets and outside the field crickets." Valerio's realistic appraisal is juxtaposed with Leonce's lyrical outburst, "Oh night, as fragrant as the first one which settled down upon paradise!" The prince craves a return to Eden, where he hopes to become one physically and consciously with nature. After eating the forbidden fruit, man gained objective awareness of himself and recognized his state of nakedness, his isolation, his wretched terrestrial lot. Ignorance was indeed bliss. If only he could go back!

But perhaps there is a way. "Death is the most blessed of dreams." It offers a possible new dimension, the ultimate and final escape from *la condition humaine*. Before the fall, man was not conscious of death, being part of nature, but subsequent to the expulsion, God sentenced him to toil, pain, and death. Here Büchner presents paradise in reverse. Through the dream-love-death experience, man hopes to regain the original perfection and harmony.

"Thus let me be your angel of death!" exclaims Leonce and kisses Lena. This embrace unites both love and death. "Too much! Too much! My whole being is in the one moment. Now die! More is impossible." Although love represents the culminating experience of life, it is swiftly followed by an anticlimax since nothing more seems possible except death itself. Only Valerio's intervention and wit appear to prevent a suicide by drowning, but the episode is ridiculed as an heroic pose by Leonce himself.

> VALERIO: Console yourself! If you don't sleep to-night as well *under* the lawn, at least you'll sleep *on top of it*. It would be an equally suicidal attempt to want to go to sleep in one of the beds. You lie on the straw like a dead man, and you'll be bitten by the fleas like a live one.
>
> LEONCE: What do I care. (He lies down on the grass.) Hey, you've just deprived me of the most beautiful suicide. Never again in my life shall I find such an opportune moment to do it, and the weather is so splendid. Now I'm no longer in the mood. That guy has ruined everything for me with his yellow vest and his sky-blue trousers.—May heaven grant me a truly healthy, sound sleep!
>
> VALERIO: Amen!—And I've saved a human life and I'll keep my body warm tonight with my good conscience.
>
> LEONCE: Your health, Valerio!

The last act of *Leonce and Lena* points to the positive effects the confrontation brings about in Leonce. "Do you also know, Valerio, that even the least significant of men is so great that life is still much too short to be able to love him?" The actual reference has superficially been inspired by Lena, whom Leonce believes to be of lowly birth. However, taken out of context, one cannot but hear Büchner, the humanist speaking. Leonce seems to have found a new directive, a reason for living brought about by his love for Lena. Some people, he remarks, imagine that they can establish a more sacred or just society and strive to this end, thus abandoning all hope of immediate joy. "A certain pleasure lies in this dear arrogance. Why should I begrudge it them?"

The arrogance of the idealist who feels that he alone can save the world finds forgiveness, for Büchner could very well have had himself in mind when he wrote these lines. Valerio once again prevents his master from losing sight of the more pragmatic approach. "Very humane and philobestial!" Not only does Büchner point out the benevolent side of the individual but he also recognizes and allows for the bestial, the self-centered animal.

As was customary for the traditional comedy of the period, *Leonce and Lena* concludes with a wedding. But in the marriage ceremony, the theme of the Garden of Eden again makes an appearance in Valerio's statement: "Well done, short and sweet, thus the little man and his miss are finally created, and all the animals of paradise stand about them." Since both main protagonists wear masks and are unknown to each other, they are still part of a puppetlike fantastic world. The creation of the universe, "short and sweet," is equally as miraculous as the new-found happiness of the two lovers. "Well, Lena, I believe it was the escape into paradise."

As the drama draws to a close, the Governess remains true to character: "A wandering prince! Now I shall die at peace." King Peter, leaving the stage in a blaze of idiocy, devotes his life to "uninterrupted thinking." Leonce, however, remains fully aware of the dramatic illusion. On a higher level, the comedy

with the masks, the stereotyped roles, and the im-
probable, conventional plot, connotes the puppet play
of life. We simply fail to see the strings. "[Tomor-
row] we shall begin the entertainment once more
from the beginning in all peace and comfort." The
monotony and boredom of perpetual repetition,
underlined by romantic irony, lessen the joy of a
questionable happy ending. "Well, Lena, do you now
see how we have our pockets full, full of dolls and
toys?" Ministers and the task of governing provide
harmless amusements. Since nothing monumental can
be achieved, should one continue with the farce of
ruling?

Valerio, the wise fool and the newly appointed
"minister of state," has the last word. "[Anyone] who
boasts of eating his bread in the sweat of his brow will
be declared insane and dangerous to human society."
According to *The Hessian Messenger, Danton's Death*
and *Woyzeck*, the state has been organized in such a
fashion that the people are obliged to work themselves
to death. Valerio advocates a complete reversal. His
paradise, consisting of idleness, melons, figs, and "a
comfortable religion" in the epicurean tradition cannot
be taken seriously. But ridiculous and ironical though
it may be, this speech implies the underlying fate of
man. Is it not tragic that both human and physical nature will not permit even a limited variation of the
utopian dream?

Since *Leonce and Lena* is the most conventional of
Büchner's dramas, because of its division into acts and
scenes and its stereotyped, fairy-tale plot, the most
traditional in its borrowings from Shakespeare and the
commedia dell'arte, and the most contemporary in its

indebtedness to German romanticism (Clemens Brentano's *Ponce de Leon*, 1801) and to Alfred de Musset (*Fantasio*, 1834), it was not surprisingly the first to be performed. But like all of Büchner's works, it has been the source of considerable debate ranging from its poetic merits, a point on which the literary critics would seem to be divided, to its theatrical interpretation. Some have dwelled upon the political content, underlining the social satire motivated by Büchner's compassionate concern for the people in their wretched material lot, while others, in more recent times, have seen in the play's exposure of the ludicrous aspects of life an anticipation of the theater of the absurd.

The rather unpromising introduction of Büchner's comedy to the stage occurred on 31 May 1885 in a park in Munich. Attendance was on a by-invitation-only basis, and the audience consisted primarily of artists and writers. The director, Ernst von Wolzogen, who also played the part of King Peter, singled out the light, joyful side of the comedy, while overlooking the more serious connotations. Indeed, a picnic atmosphere was created as can be ascertained in the report of Max Halbe, who assumed the role of Leonce. "In some bushes to the side [of the stage] there was a barrel of beer placed upon a trestle in order not to let our guests go thirsty during the intermission. Thus, not only art but also throat and stomach were cared for in the best Munich tradition; our show could begin."[2]

Since the entertainment had to be interrupted on account of darkness, the spectators were served beer and bread rolls as emergency arrangements were made. Finally, the third act, played by lantern light, enjoyed an enthusiastic reception, no doubt aided by the refreshments. Despite the favorable impression it left, this intimate production contributed little to making Büchner well known in the European theater.

The real credit for having initiated a *Leonce and Lena* renaissance must go to the Vienna Residenztheater production of 30 December 1911. It was offered in the afternoon as part of a program to revive interest in writers who deserved to be recognized. Consequently, the main concern of the director, Ludwig Wolf, was to secure popular acceptance, once again at the expense of the serious undercurrent, by exaggerating the comic element to create "a circus comedy."[3] It follows that Karl Etlinger as Valerio stole the show. Most critics considered the performance as an event of only literary significance. Whereas the *Neue Freie Presse* opposed and the *Neues Wiener Journal* generally supported this revival, solely the *Wiener Arbeiterzeitung* gave the staging its enthusiastic endorsement. But, quite obviously, the theatergoing public was becoming increasingly aware of Georg Büchner.

A 1912 version by the Düsseldorf Bühne, intended as the evening's main attraction, marked the acknowledgement and appreciation of the play's dramatic merit. The director, Gustav Lindemann, endeavoured to remain faithful to Büchner's concept by emphasizing the lyrical sections. Although he successfully reproduced a dream-world aura, he avoided a tendency to romanticize, in part realized by Eugen Dumont's interpretation of Valerio as the realistic side of Büchner. Eduard Sturm's sets deserve special note. A dark-violet foreground supplied a screen in which an oval had been cut. Separated from the theatrical realm of illusion by the dark frame, the audience could view a fairyland in muted colors by means of the oval aperture, as if they were gazing through a magic window upon what the *Hamburger Fremden-blatt* called "an excerpt from the country of Fantasia."[4] As in most subsequent productions of *Leonce and Lena*, music, composed in this instance by Hans Schindler, contributed significantly to the lyrical vein of the acting and to the smooth transition from scene to scene.

On 17 December 1913, the Berlin Lessingtheater celebrated a Büchner evening with stagings of both *Woyzeck* and *Leonce and Lena*. An effort was made to steer a middle course between the lyrical, dreamy Düsseldorf version and the exaggeratedly comic, loud-colored Viennese rendition. Reviewing the Berlin interpretation, Herbert Ihering observed:

> The world is not denied, but it has become play. And nowhere does Büchner's artistry become brighter and gayer than when, in a blasé and pessimistic fashion, he mocks the world's institutions. This mockery is purified of the last polemical remnant and still contains an element in which clumsy philistines and dim-witted kings become free and dance. The Lessingtheater, which is in the process of building up an excellent repertoire, had [Karl] Walser design the sets. Thus arose, at least for the nature scenes, a sensually light-hearted, coquettishly melancholy world in which the figures were placed with ironic fantasy.[5]

All of the interpretations before World War I either passed over or played down the social-critical note. However, a theater scandal erupted on 2 June 1918 in Mannheim where Richard Weichert presented

Leonce and Lena as a satire on absolutism and the governing mentality of petty states, a particularly sensitive issue in the concluding year of the war. Even the Church objected, especially in the person of Pastor Paul Klein, who spoke out against the production in a sermon and in an open letter sent to the *Mannheimer Generalanzeiger*. Although there is a social comment in the comedy, it would nonetheless be a case of arbitrary exaggeration to classify Büchner exclusively as a poet of political protest, and, as was the case with *Danton's Death*, he became the unwitting victim of an overzealous, politically committed director.

Still another form of overstatement could be witnessed in the Berlin Staatliche Schauspielhaus on 16 December 1921. Cutting all the grotesque, absurd references as well as the more serious, realistic elements, Karl Bruck concentrated upon recreating an innocuous fairy tale, an impression reinforced by the décor and costumes. Indeed, the noted critic Alfred Kerr referred to the performance as a fashion show,[6] totally lacking in verve despite the excellent music by Carl Orff. There was also a serious casting problem: Karl Etlinger's crudely humorous depiction of Valerio (he played the same role in Vienna, 1911) clashed severely with the saccharine sweetness of the lovers enacted by Lothar Müthel, Leonce, and Annemarie Seidel, Lena.

The years 1923 to 1927, which saw several stagings of *Leonce and Lena* in the German-speaking countries, basically continued this fairy-tale trend. Typical of this approach was the Hamburg Kammerspiele rendering of September 1925, in which Lena, played by Herta Wildschild was described as "a delicate princess figurine surrounded by moonlight."[7] However, the utilization of actors dressed as pages to set up the necessary properties before each scene constituted one noteworthy innovation. The other extreme, the social revolutionary note, came to the fore again in April 1926 in the Akademietheater in Vienna. A one-act play written in praise of the Emperor Franz Joseph preceded *Leonce and Lena*, which director Hans Brahm interpreted as a satire on the monarchy, achieved by underscoring the realistic, parodistic side of the comedy. To assure a more up-to-date understanding and thus to remove the comfortable cushion of historical distance, he had his actors wear more contemporary costumes and accompanied the action with modern incidental music. When King Peter made his stage appearance to the strains of "Hail to you in the victor's wreath," the national anthem of imperial Germany, a near riot broke out in the audience, and only with difficulty could the hecklers be silenced and the performance be concluded. The local press concentrated more upon discovering the identity of the troublemakers, but in the process credence was once more given undeservedly to the social-revolutionary label.

During the 1920s, the Nazis viewed the writer of *The Hessian Messenger* and the darling of many left-wing artists and intellectuals with considerable suspicion. But despite political disqualification, Büchner continued to be performed after 1933 under the new regime. Directors were, of course, obliged to adhere to the realistic element and promote the drama as an historic document of the nineteenth century, with strict avoidance of any allusion to the present political situation. As a consequence, *Leonce and Lena* suffered from its double billing with Kleist's *Broken Jug* in the Berlin Volksbühne in February 1934, for Heinz Hilpert tried unsuccessfully to accommodate Büchner's play to the more down-to-earth tone of the peasant comedy. Through satire and parody, a caricature of the petty little state in action was revealed. Leonce appeared in the first scene lying upon a bed, playing with a yoyo hanging from a little crown. In singling out the light, humorous side, Hilpert chose to ignore the tragic implications. Whereas one of the Nazi-controlled papers rejected the drama since it did not provide "strength through joy,"[8] another went to great lengths to prove that Büchner would be in support of the National Socialist cause. Now, both left and right-wing political groups had claimed him as their own.

In June 1957, the Freie Volksbühne of the Kurfürstendamm Theater, Berlin, traveled to England for a guest performance at Sadler's Wells. Generally, the *Leonce and Lena* staging found little favor with the critic of the London *Times*, who felt that the actors had taken "a flatteringly serious view of their culture mission to London."[9] The review dwells to a considerable degree upon the modernity of Büchner's drama and tends to evaluate the interpretation in this light. "The comedy is relatively a slight matter, but even that has curious affinities with the theatre of Anouilh." The acting (Leonce—Maximilian Schell, Lena—Marion Degler, and Valerio—Bruno Dallansky) lacked vigor; and the production was regarded as "an allegorical contrast between age and youth."

The one aspect selected for special praise was the stage décor created by perhaps the most famous set designer of Büchner's plays, especially *Danton's Death*. "Caspar Neher's setting of folding screens discreetly and evocatively presenting atmospheric pictures is a continued delight and the costumes and the makeup bring out the lifelessness of the king and his court as the background which youth finds so boring."

There was a concerted attempt to acquaint England with Georg Büchner in the 1950s as further evidenced by the 59 Theater Company production at the Royal Court Theater in April 1959, executed by final-year drama students and young professionals. In his program notes to the comedy, the director and translator Michael Geliot designated Büchner as a precursor "of Brechtian epic drama."[10] Although *Leonce and Lena*, being written in the traditional mold as a parody of that specific tradition, could hardly be said to fit Brecht's concept of the open-ended play, Geliot, said the London *Times*, "was determined to see the resemblance and went resolutely to work, giving his translation a punchy modernism".[11] Hence his version proved reminiscent of the one-sided political interpretations beginning with the Mannheim staging of 1918. Since Leonce's dilemma was only peripherally alluded to, the role, interpreted by Michael Davies, failed to convey a well-defined or memorable impression and Bill Wallis as Valerio, "the philosopher of the belly . . . gave a display of uproarious comic realism"[12] more in keeping with a Brechtian comic figure.

In the context of the French avant-garde, *Leonce and Lena* came to be regarded as a significant forerunner of surrealism in its absurd presentation of courtly routine and ceremony and in its depiction of a decadent individual for whom "death is the most blessed dream" and for whom love is only a means to temporarily overcome a Baudelairean "spleen." The Théâtre Franco-Allemand from Paris demonstrated this tendency in June 1961 at the Ludwigsburg Summer Festival. The creator and director of the group, Wolfram Mehring, made extensive use of gesture and thus fashioned a dramatic style in which mime and mask contributed significantly to the spoken word.

The court scenes became exercises in pantomime as the speeches were emitted from loudspeakers and actions were accompanied by electronic music, which reinforced the bizarre atmosphere. Since all minor figures wore masks and their speeches originated exclusively from the loudspeakers, they seemed, so to speak, alienated. Only Leonce, Lena, and Valerio actually spoke their lines. Mehring himself played Leonce while Grillon, who also designed the masks and costumes, put forward a contrast figure in his Valerio. "Not only the individual figure but also the groups were conceived choreographically as dancing sculpture. Harpsichord music ("La Folia" and other Baroque sounds) joined the scenes and a happy, optic-acoustic harmony resulted" (Winfried Wild).[13] The performance, offered in the afternoon in German and at night in French, was widely acclaimed.

"The comedy *Leonce and Lena*, one of the most lovable exceptions of the German theater, does not originate with Samuel Beckett, not even with August Strindberg. This must be particularly stated after Hans Schalla's new staging in the Bochum Kammerspiele" (Heinz Beckmann).[14] The French absurdist influence can be readily ascertained in this 1963 production, which stood under the influence of Beckett's *Endgame*. This strange version, simply designated "Three Acts by Georg Büchner," i.e., denying it the title of a comedy, concentrated upon the note of decadence and decay especially underlined by Herbert Scherreiks's sets intended to represent mold and spider webs. The actors, who also doubled as stage hands, limped across the stage and created the impression that they could well fall asleep at any moment. Liesel Alex portrayed Lena as a somnambulistic old maid of fifty, a characterization which the casting emphasized by juxtaposing her with a considerably younger Governess. Obviously, very much under the spell of Beckett, Schalla elected to focus on one aspect of Büchner to the detriment of the lighter side of the comedy. The critic Beckmann, who generally felt that this experiment proved unsuccessful, drew special attention to the scene where Valerio introduces the masked Leonce and Lena as mechanical puppets, an episode pointed to by the Avant-Garde as an anticipation of "modern existential consciousness."[15] Here, however, because of all the previous yawning and general decay, the incident became a mere extension or confirmation of a message announced as soon as the curtain was raised.

The year 1968 produced several approaches to Büchner's comedy. These included a "subversive reportage"[16] technique offered by a small private Frankfurt theater, Die Katakombe, in which quotations from Büchner and from contemporary political figures formed part of an attack against German political narrow-mindedness and the first Zürich production since 1919 under the direction of Rolf Henniger, who avoided crass comic effects or theatrical acrobatics in favor of a discreet, uniform plan in keeping with a close reading of Büchner. But perhaps the most intriguing performance took place in the Munich Puppet Theater, which celebrated its twentieth anniversary with a *Leonce and Lena* première. The basic plot with its prince and princess, the escape, the chance encounter, and the "happy ending" are, of course, the stuff that marionette performances are made of. Hence the director (as well as producer, writer, puppet carver, puppeteer, set designer, and speaker) Herbert Fischel opted to accentuate the idyllic, fairy-tale aspect in order to create a "poetic miniature world"[17] at the exclusion of the melancholy, satiric, and absurd content. The evening amounted to a puppeteering tour de force as Fischel and his two colleagues provided not only the manipulation but also the required voices for their respective hand puppets.

During the 1969 theatrical season in Vienna, the Volkstheater presented *Leonce and Lena* together with *Woyzeck* in a rendering which stressed above all Büchner's feeling for life, the background of monotony and despair which many directors have ignored or given only fleeting reference to. Director Rudolf Kautek successfully brought to the stage the human dilemma described by Werner Bökenkamp in the program notes. "Leonce like Lenz and before him Danton, plagued by a terrible boredom, parodies himself, transforms himself into his own clown, into the comedian of his own fate. In this sense his servant, a descendant of the classical Harlequin, has been given depth and has been grotesquely intensified. He expresses the impossibility of communication or understanding by fantastic mimicry and crazy madness which is aware of itself."[18] As a comedy dealing with tedium and stressing the futility of action, the performance tended to bog down in sheer ennui itself as incarnated by Albert Rolant's Leonce, but Herbert Propst, who also played Woyzeck the same evening, contributed to the inevitable forward motion with his

LEONCE (Albert Rolant): Arise in your white dress and walk behind the corpse through the night and sing it its death song!
LENA (Kitty Speiser): Who speaks there?
LEONCE: A dream.
LENA: Dreams are blessed.
LEONCE: Then dream yourself blessed and let me be your blessed dream.
LENA: Death is the most blessed dream.
LEONCE: Then let me be your angel of death! Let my lips sink down upon your eyes like the angel of death's wings.

The climax of the comedy is reached as Leonce kisses Lena.
HELMUT BAAR, VIENNA

pragmatic, crudely humorous interpretation of Valerio.

Writing for *The Times*, 1 September 1971, Michael Billington gave a most enthusiastic review of the Bulandra Theater of Bucharest production of *Leonce and Lena* for the Edinburgh Festival. The director,

Liviu Ciulei, sought to demonstrate Büchner's modernity in a somewhat selective "theatrical patchwork quilt matching numerous contemporary acting and production styles to the dramatist's allusive text."[19] A Brechtian prologue during which the actors could be seen limbering up, a Leonce and Valerio reminiscent of Beckett's tramps, or a King Peter playing with plastic ducks in his bath tub recalling Planchon's *The Three Musketeers* were some of the more obvious patches; and "yet Ciulei's palimpsest of a production [was] held together by its own organic vitality and partly by a towering central performance by Ion Caranitru as Leonce."[20] Opening in New York, March 1974, this same production marked the American debut of *Leonce and Lena*. As Clive Barnes wrote for the *New York Times*, "The Arena Stage is to be congratulated for our belated Büchner première, but better still it has brought Liviu Ciulei to America for the first time. . . . He is one of the most imaginative directors in the world today, and his simple concept of *Leonce and Lena* as a sort of time capsule of world theater right up to the foolish epics of Brecht and the epic follies of Ionesco proves electric and of course eclectic."[21] As in Edinburgh, Ciulei staged an audience warm-up during which passages from all three Büchner plays were tossed about so that the audience was at somewhat of a loss when the actual performance began. The director also managed to inspire exceptional acting on the part of J. C. Jones—Valerio, Dennis Howard—Leonce, and Max Wright—King Peter.

"A radical staging of a radical comedy."[22] Thus Winfried Roesner described a very successful *Leonce and Lena* directed by Jürgen Flimm for the Mann-

heim Nationaltheater in 1973. In the last act, as the
people and the court awaited the arrival of the royal
couple, complete stillness, disconnected dialogue, a
string quartet playing in a cupboard, and the howl of a
hurricane alternated with one another, while the
actors stood motionless in the midst of a winter storm.
Flimm went to great lengths to complement the play
by a careful study of the additional fragments and
even by the inclusion of a passage from Büchner's
Lenz narrative. What at first glance may have appeared to be arbitrary choice or poetic license could
indeed be justified on the basis of the text. For example, the fascinating winter landscape was suggested
by a line from the second act. "I already see him [on
his way to the madhouse] on a wide alley, on an ice-
cold winter day."

The surrealistic sets by Hans Kleber drew special
effect from an omnipresent cupboard which served as
the King's bedroom, the chamber of state, or the interior of a tavern. The collaboration between Flimm
and the composer Jens Peter Ostendorf led to "a
meaningful expansion of stage language."[23] In a manner calling to mind the techniques Büchner resorted
to in the writing of *Leonce and Lena,* i.e., satire on
romanticism through indirect quotation, Ostendorf
wrote an original score which consisted of an adaptation of the musical language of the nineteenth century
(Schumann, Debussy, Beethoven, Smetana) and which
he himself classified as "false music in the highest degree."

Peter Brombacher's Valerio, who was depicted as a
deserter endeavoring to exploit the prince just as the
latter uses his subjects, added a political accent. However, his promotion to minister of state signaled an

ironic but resigned solution to the social issue. "What one heard and saw here in two and a half hours of performance (for thirty-five pages of text!) was an uncommonly careful construction, a 'complete work of art,' a precision apparatus for the resuscitation and release of a largely encoded text."

"Nothing speaks more for this staging than the fact that it is impossible to go into it without at the same time going into the play. Büchner's poetic text has become fully and completely theater. Word for word, syllable for syllable. That out of a text of approximately thirty to thirty-five printed pages a performance of almost three hours could be made proves how intensive Büchner's word is, how fully laden with meaning, with associations, if one wants to sound it out and realize it in a theatrically concrete form."[24] This introduction to a very positive review written by Piero Rismondo for *Die Presse* is in praise indicative of the excitement engendered by Johannes Schaaf's production of *Leonce and Lena* for the Salzburg Festival of 1975, which was not only brought back to Salzburg the following summer but was even shown on television. The immense acclaim this rendering enjoyed was attributed to "a highly intellectual penetration of the text"[25] by a director who knew his business and who recognized in his source an existential tragedy satirically presented in the decadent form of a romantic comedy. To suggest the instability of the human condition, Wilfried Minks designed a green hill which rose from the orchestra pit to a height of about half the stage. It provided some effective ascending entries and some amusing descending exits, while a system of mirrors and veils suggested the remaining necessary sets.

Court Chaplain (*composing himself*): If it please your majesty, Prince Leonce of the kingdom of Popo and if it pleases your majesty, Princess Lena of the kingdom of Pipi, if it please your majesties mutually and reciprocally to want to have and to hold one another, then speak a loud and audible Yes. Lena and Leonce. "Yes!"

Hero and heroine miraculously find one another and a questionable happy ending during the grand-finale conclusion of *Leonce and Lena* in perhaps the most celebrated production of the comedy directed by Johannes Schaaf for the Salzburg Festival of 1975 and 1976. The title roles were played by Klaus Maria Brandauer (Leonce) and Marianne Mentwich (Lena).

SALZBURGER FESTSPIELE, SALZBURG

Generally, the play proved to be exceptionally well cast, especially the role of Valerio interpreted by Peter Brogle, "a true-hearted fellow full of movement and the joy of comfortable living. When he rolls in the grass, you think you can smell the scent of the meadow. Special applause breaks out when he proves himself to be an accomplished tight-rope walker upon a steel cable, which represents the border of his kingdom [in the last scene]."[26] Famous for his "optical fantasy," Schaaf made extensive use of gestures and mime and most of the special effects, although often possessing a social or political barb, appealed directly to the eye. In order to represent visually the state of sycophancy and subservience in which the people live, Schaaf hired real midgets to impersonate the mechanical courtiers.

However, Winfried Wild felt that he went too far when Leonce (Klaus Maria Brandauer), after kissing Lena, lowered his head to the ground and stood on his head exclaiming, "Too much, too much!" or when Rosetta (Sylvia Manas) sang her parting song in a supine position while Leonce dragged her about the hill and moved her legs in time to the music. Finally, to indicate the "fatalism of history," the absurd, automatic cycle of existence, the comedy concluded not with Valerio's utopian dream but rather with a scene of Schaaf's own creation. Once Leonce and Lena had retired to a small room over which a black curtain fell, the new king was overheard babbling his father's introductory speech: "Man must think and I must think for my subjects, for they don't think."

"Good heavens, Jerome! Was that really Georg Büchner's *Leonce and Lena*? Or perhaps the great clown finale literally enriched from the Krone

Circus?"[27] The Hamburg Deutsche Schauspielhaus opened its doors in November 1975 to Jerome Savary, director and "inventor"[28] of the Parisian "Grand Magic Circus," who transformed Büchner's comedy into a "macabre fairy-tale in bright colors,"[29] a montage review including the carnival scene from *Woyzeck* and quotations ranging from the commedia dell' arte to the musical. In the first scene, Valerio entered from the audience and then proceeded to bite the buttocks of a naked woman lying about the stage, a remnant of the introductory orgy. Lena was portrayed as a sleeping beauty complete with her evil fairy, Peter as the frog king, and Leonce as a sad clown who at one point took a bath in Snow White's glass coffin.

This compilation of extravagant circus numbers which chose to ignore Büchner's real strength, the spoken word, managed to entertain the audience but also to annoy or outrage most of the critics, one of whom wrote: "In short, that Parisian devil is a bad ignoramus . . . a theatrical pyromaniac" (Horst Ziermann).[30] As if in keeping with the cyclical view of life propounded in the last scene of *Leonce and Lena*, we have made a complete revolution back to the "circus comedy" noted by a critic who reviewed the first significant performance of December 1911 in the Vienna Residenztheater.

5. WOYZECK

Woyzeck does not act, he is acted upon. While shaving his Captain, he must tolerate ridicule and moral criticism from his superior officer. "You have a child without the blessing of the church." The Doctor uses him as a guinea pig in an experiment designed to prove by a strictly controlled diet the supposed superiority of man over beast. The fact that "subject Woyzeck" has eaten nothing but peas and water for several months helps to explain his hallucinatory apocalyptic vision in an open field.

> WOYZECK: Yes, Andres, that streak there across the grass, that's where the head rolls in the evening. Once someone picked it up, he thought it was a hedgehog. Three days and three nights and he lay upon woodshavings in his coffin. (*Softly*) Andres, it was the Freemasons. I've got it, the Freemasons. Listen!
> ANDRES (*sings*): *There sat two hares and*
> *Ate up the green, green grass . . .*
> WOYZECK: Listen! It's up to something!
> ANDRES: *Ate up the green, green grass*
> *Right to the ground.*
> WOYZECK: It's moving behind me, under me (*stamps on the ground*). Hollow, don't you

hear it? Everything's hollow down there. The Freemasons!

ANDRES: I'm scared.

WOYZECK: It's so strangely still. You're tempted to hold your breath. Andres!

ANDRES: What?

WOYZECK: Say something! (*stares at the country-side*) Andres! Look how bright it is! A fire flames about the heavens and a thundering noise roars down like trumpets. It's getting closer! Let's go! Don't look behind you. (*Drags him into the bush.*)

ANDRES (*after a pause*): Woyzeck! Do you still hear it?

WOYZECK: Silent, everything silent, as if the world was dead.

ANDRES: Hey, listen! They're drumming in town. We've got to go.

To compound his misfortune, his common-law wife Marie is being hotly pursued by the animalistic Drum Major who admires her physical attributes at the town fair. "What a broad! . . . Hell, just right for the propagation of dragoon regiments and the breeding of drum majors!" Woyzeck has an early indication of his wife's betrayal: he catches her admiring a gift of gold earrings. But he is only made fully aware of his domestic misfortune when the Doctor and the Captain sadistically bait him with Marie's infidelity. "Captain, sir, I'm a poor devil and I've got nothing else in the world. Captain, if you're joking" Woyzeck's little world of suffering begins to crumble.

As an outsider looking in through the window of a local tavern, he observes Marie dancing with the Drum Major: "Round and round, round and round!" Pursued by the incessantly pounding rhythm of the dance, he flees to an open field where he hears a voice:

"Stab, stab the bitch wolf to death! . . . I keep on hearing it, round and round, stab to death, to death!" Once he has suffered a humiliating defeat at the hands of his rival in a wrestling match ("One thing after another"), Woyzeck purchases a knife from a Jew and gives away his earthly possessions. Briefly the scene switches to Marie. She is reading the Bible and draws a parallel between her dilemma and that of the adulterous woman forgiven by Christ.

In response to the homicidal imperative, Woyzeck takes Marie outside the town, where he proceeds to stab her fatally. "Take that and that! Can't you die? And that! and that! Ha, she's still moving. Not dead yet, not dead yet? Still alive? (continues to stab). Are you dead? Dead! Dead!"

Later, confronted with the telltale blood upon his arm at the tavern, he escapes to the scene of the crime and casts the knife into a pond. In one version of the play, he is last seen wading into the water, looking for the incriminating weapon, and trying to wash away the bloodstains. At the inquest the court clerk remarks, "A good murder, a genuine murder, a beautiful murder, as beautiful as you could ever wish for. It's a long time since we've had such a good one."

On 27 August 1824, in the market square in Leipzig, a large crowd gathered to witness the public decapitation of Wolfgang Johann Christian Woyzeck who, after having been declared sane and answerable for his actions, was to be executed in compliance with the demands of the law. The "Woyzeck case," as it came to be known, was fully investigated and reviewed in the report of Johann Christian Clarus, who treated the life and death of the psychopathic barber-soldier as a moral treatise, warning youth of the dangers inherent in laziness, drunkenness, gambling, and sexual license.

This particular incident gained much interest and publicity at the time. The major issue, hotly debated in legal and medical circles, was whether or not Woyzeck could be held responsible for the murder of the rather disreputable Leipzig prostitute Frau Woostin. Clarus and the medical faculty felt, however, that despite this dissolute life and macabre, pseudoreligious visions, his crime was the result of uncontrolled passion, jealousy, and weakness of will. Approximately ten years later, in his father's library, Büchner was to come upon Clarus's report, which provided him with the barest external structure for his tragedy. The drama fulfills Büchner's basic aesthetic demand of remaining true to reality, but Büchner revealed his genius in the reconstruction and reinterpretation of the given facts in accordance with his own essentially pessimistic view of life. His creative energy is centered primarily in the portrayal of types and characters, such as the simpleminded Andres, the bombastic Drum Major, and, above all, Marie and Woyzeck, in whose personalities no trace of their prototypes can be ascertained.

In what has been called "the definitive monograph on Büchner,"[1] Karl Viëtor maintains that this drama has been constructed on a revolutionary new basis.[2] From the very onset, Woyzeck is made to suffer patiently and passively; pain and degradation constitute the very fabric of his existence. Viëtor contradicts the socialist interpreter who sees the main issue as the class struggle, for the hero is not meant to incarnate a purely social or revolutionary accusation against the powers of society which mock, scorn, and sap his life's strength. The Captain and the Doctor form only part of the cruel powers which lead to Woyzeck's martyrdom and destruction. He is poor, abused, inarticulate, overstrained, but above all he is in love with Marie and deeply devoted to her.

Despite his ugliness and degradation, Woyzeck's character still possesses a certain dignity in its naturalness and truthfulness. To underline the reality, the innate living qualities of the lower class, his personality is set off against the artificial sentimentality and morality of the Captain and the cold ruthlessness of the Doctor, caricatures representing a static, convention-bound alien world which surrounds and persecutes Woyzeck.

In her introduction to an English school edition,[3] Margaret Jacobs places more emphasis upon the human element in Woyzeck's tragedy. Despite a materialistic senseless existence, the protagonist rises above the social straitjacket in his all-consuming love for Marie and his child. For them he bears without complaint the burdens and exploitations of his tormentors, since the loved ones alone give his life a sense of importance. Already under excessive mental strain as a result of the Doctor's inhuman experiments and faced with the loss of those he loves, Woyzeck sees his world start to collapse. In the last resort, the final calamity does not depend entirely upon social conditions subject to change, but rather on certain immutable aspects of human nature. After discovering his rival, Woyzeck displays an overwhelming sense of loneliness, bewilderment, and jealousy at losing all in Marie.

It is also of interest to note Benno von Wiese's interpretation of the supernatural or psychological elements which he explains in terms of "original fear" (*Urangst*), the distress of existence.[4] Man is arbitrarily placed into creation, and in his createdness he sees himself opposite the anonymous—the realm of secret omens and wonders. "Doctor, have you ever seen any sign of double nature? When the sun stands still at noon and it's almost as if the world were being consumed in fire, a terrible voice spoke to me!" His phobia cannot be attributed to a specific object, but is rooted in being itself. This original fear before the incomprehensible undermines his feeling of security with the result that he is persecuted by images usually in some relationship to the world of natural phenomena. This explains Woyzeck's pathological obsession with the "it," the fear of an insecure, shelterless existence. "It followed behind me all the way to the town. What's to become of it?" Of course, in such a view the ideas of sin and guilt deducible from a rational world order become meaningless. Man can only stand struck with awe and horror in the presence of the infathomable which gradually invades, tyrannizes, and enslaves his innermost being.

The theme of suffering is the subject of a specialized chapter entitled "A World of Suffering, Georg Büchner," written by J. P. Stern.[5] Investigating Büchner from primarily a psychological point of view, Stern feels that Büchner's writings constitute an image of life "valid as a momentous exaggeration"[6] arising from his own unfortunate career. Stern's most significant contribution to Büchner criticism, however, lies in the indication and conclusive substantiation of suffering as the underlying preoccupation in his plays and short story. "The experience fundamental to Büchner's vision of human character and destiny, and the unifying theme of his literary work, are the experience and the theme of the world under the aspect of suffering."[7]

A more restrictive approach looks upon the play as

a milieu drama of social determinism much in the manner of the late nineteenth-century naturalists. This point of view is best represented by Hans Mayer. In his study,[8] the true motive for Woyzeck's crime can be found in his poverty, the circumstances of his material existence, into which he was irrevocably born. "Nature just makes us that way, but if I was a gentleman and had a hat and a watch and a formal coat and could talk elegant, I'd sure want to be virtuous. Virtue must be a beautiful thing, Captain, but I'm only a poor guy." Both his behavior and that of his persecutors are seen as the products of environment. Difference in social level leads to difference in opinion as to morals and customs, while fortune and advancement are solely reserved for those born into the right class. The question is raised as to what is the nature and power of these social conditions, who establishes them and who can change them if man cannot. Mayer correctly recognizes that in the last analysis Büchner's world must be considered in terms of pessimistic fatalism since man is powerless to alter the course of life.

There can be no doubt that Büchner experienced excessive bitterness at the injustice of the social order, but having gained insight into the immutable laws of being, he renounced any hope in political revolution or the creation of any type of utopia. The most radical sociological interpretation can be found in Georg Lukács's critical study.[9] Influenced by Marxist theory and his desire to distinguish between "the George Büchner falsified by the Fascists and the real Georg Büchner," he tries to portray him as a purely "plebeian revolutionary in whom the economic foundations for a liberation of the working masses are beginning to crystalize."[10] Lukács's work is valuable as an indication of the degree to which Büchner anticipated Marx's materialistic interpretation of the historical process, but in his failure to recognize Büchner's complete disillusionment with revolution, or, for that matter, with any human action as a means to create a more just social order, he tends to distort the facts of the play to fit his preconceived notion.

Historically oriented critics who have made a study of the transitional period at the beginning of the nineteenth century tend to favor a nihilistic analysis of *Woyzeck*. Many young intellectuals of this new generation were caught in the grips of a painful dissonance, torn between the still dominant but fading classical-romantic idealism and the recent doctrines of materialism. As Ludwig Büttner aptly sums up: "What the nineteenth century was to develop, its disjointed and tragic view of life, the seeds of this could already be found in Büchner."[11] Seeing the traditional values laid bare as mere appearance and having no access to a satisfying substitute, these disillusioned young men gave expression to nihilistic concepts of life. That such elements exist in *Woyzeck* cannot be denied (the black fairy tale). Viëtor, for example, identifies primarily in *Woyzeck* the will of its author who, with harsh decisiveness, penetrates the heart-warming illusion of life to unveil the void within, the true god of our world for those with the courage to be honest with themselves.

The materialist philosopher Ludwig Feuerbach once wrote: "Man is what he eats."[12] Most critics have failed to take into consideration the importance of the experiment in animal metabolism conducted by the Doctor and the extent to which it is conducive to the

GRANDMOTHER: Once upon a time there was a poor child and he had no father and no mother. Everything was dead and there was no one left on the earth. Everything dead, and he went and cried day and night. And since there was no one else on earth, he wanted to go to heaven, and the moon looked at him so friendly and when at last he reached the moon, it was a piece of rotten wood and then he went to the sun and when he got to the sun, it was a withered sunflower and when he reached the stars, they were little gold flies which were stuck up there just like the shrike sticks them on thorns, and when he wanted to return to earth, the earth was an upturned pot and he was completely alone and he sat down and cried and there he still sits and is completely alone.

This black fairy tale has often been pointed to as a concise expression of Büchner's pessimistic, nihilistically oriented view of existence. In the famous Teatro Stabile Torino production of Woyzeck (1970–71), Isa Falleni Trofarelli portrayed the grandmother.

TEATRO STABILE DI TORINO

tragedy in *Woyzeck*. In physiological terms, the pure pea diet renders Woyzeck an exhausted, emaciated shadow of a man who has lost his vitality. He is subject to muscle spasms, his hair has begun to fall out, and his eyesight fails him on occasion. Unable to find physical satisfaction with her husband, Marie falls an easy prey to the sensual Drum Major.

A state of semistarvation often causes abnormal mental activity, such as hallucinations, which in Woyzeck's case serve further to alienate him from his wife, who is overcome by fear and apprehension at her husband's eccentric and irregular life. The Drum Major, in his animal simplicity, represents a more secure, assured way of life than that of a man who appears to ignore his own child. "He didn't even look at his kid." Since Woyzeck is already under excessive mental and physical strain derived from the imposed diet, discovery of a rival gives rise to a complete psychological upheaval. In such a chaotic emotional state, disappointment, jealousy, and revenge are transformed by a previously overexerted psyche into a homicidal imperative, rationalized as an external tyrannical force subjugating the defenseless mind of the individual. "Stab, stab the bitch wolf dead! Should I? Must I?"

In direct contrast to this positivistic approach, other critics place some emphasis upon a religious explanation of the play. Woyzeck refers to Marie's infidelity as a "sin," and, after her fall, she appeals to God to help her to resist desire.

> MARIA (*leafs through the Bible*): Neither was guile found in his mouth"—Lord God! Lord God! Don't look at me! (*turns some more pages*). "And the scribes and Pharisees brought unto him a woman taken in adultery; and when

they had set her in the midst.—And Jesus said unto her, Neither do I condemn thee: go, and sin no more." (*Marie claps her hands together.*) Lord God! Lord God! I can't! Lord God, just give me enough strength so I can pray. (*The child nestles up to her.*) The child gives me a stab in the heart. Karl! My sin's as glaring as the sun!

FOOL (*is lying down and telling himself stories on his fingers.*) He's got the golden crown, his majesty the king. Tomorrow I'll fetch her majesty's child. Blood sausage says: come, liver sausage! (*He takes the child and remains quiet.*)

MARIE: Franz hasn't come, not yesterday, not to-day. It's gettin' hot here.

(*She opens the window.*)

"And stood at his feet behind him weeping, and began to wash his feet with tears, and did wipe them with the hairs of her head, and kissed his feet, and anoint them with the ointment" (*beats her breast*). Everything dead! Savior, Savior, I only wish I could anoint your feet!"

A fear or presentiment that God's will is also at work in the universe is evident in Woyzeck's apocalyptic vision, reminiscent of an Old-Testament-judging God. "Andres, look how bright it is! A fire flames about the heavens and a thundering noise roars down like trumpets." The constant mention of the devil is not accidental and underscores a naive sense of religion. Franz Mautner points out the parallel between "Savior" in the scene in which Marie reads the Bible and the pious verses "Lord, as your body red and sore,/ So let my heart be ever more" in the following scene.[13] It is thus intimated that Woyzeck, in giving away his worldly goods and accepting his burden of suffering, assumes Christlike proportions. Fear of the

Lord may pervade the dramatic atmosphere, but salvation one can discover no trace of. In an absurd world, the power of love still exists, although it may destroy its object. The tragedy of *Woyzeck* would seem to repudiate and damn a godless world in which such love is impossible.

One of the most extensive examinations of Marie's character, its predecessors and its originality, was conducted by Viëtor.[14] As proof of Büchner's creative and inventive powers, he first indicates that there is no similarity between Marie and her historical model. She stands out as a child of nature in the tradition of Goethe's Gretchen, but with a significant difference. Although it is evident that Gretchen served Büchner as a source of inspiration, one is equally conscious of the stark naturalistic realism of Marie, which surpasses Goethe's more sentimentalized portrayal. Completely lacking the naive innocence of the *Faust* model, Marie seeks to gratify her sexual appetite. Viëtor consequently glorifies her as the living incarnation of the supremacy and superiority of nature over the hypocrisy and hollowness of middle-class morality. In the light of the victimizing power of sex over Marie, it would be incompatible with the events and the final impression of the drama to present nature as a purely positive force.

Whereas the representatives of the people are depicted with affection and understanding by the creator in a naturalistic style, a completely different method of presentation is employed to set off the despised persecutors of the people, that of the caricature, a literary weapon which aims to disclose and undermine the despicable through derision. Wolfgang Martens in his article "Caricature in Büchner's Works" has made the most thorough contribution to the study of the Captain.[15] The latter incarnates the perfect image of the officer and narrow-minded philistine who has assumed all the self-centered views and habits of a typical bourgeois. In his indifference to Woyzeck's fate, he epitomizes an inhuman representative of society who hides himself in a meaningless conviction of the good and the noble:

> CAPTAIN: Woyzeck, you've got no virtue. You're not a virtuous man. Flesh and blood? When I lie at the window when it's rained and let my eyes follow the white stockings as they jump across the alleys—damn it all, Woyzeck— then I feel love. I also have flesh and blood. But Woyzeck, virtue, virtue! How should I fill in my time then? I always say to myself: you are a virtuous man (moved), a good man, a good man.

Such a stance protects his delicate feelings from the dark reality of human distress, while at the same time it enables him to indulge in an artificial form of sentimentality. In his psychological makeup there are signs of the ultimate decay and decline of the middle class. He constantly shows evidence of a strange nervousness, timidity, and unrest, very unbourgeois qualities for a class that insists upon order, regularity, and stability. Like many of Büchner's characters, he suffers from the fear of existence itself and the characteristic malady of his class, boredom, symptomatic of a hollow, artificial, and superficial way of life, a malignant growth gradually eating away his natural vitality.

The caricature of the Doctor, as Viëtor indicates, found its inspiration in Wilbrand, one of Büchner's Giessen professors.[16] Destruction by ridicule is called upon a pseudo-scientist who speaks of "pissing on the wall" and who entertains the convictions that his tendency to sneeze serves science and that a pulse rate of sixty indicates self-control. In his unsuccessful experiment devised to demonstrate man's free will and hence superiority over the animal kingdom, he fails to recognize the laws of common human decency. Woyzeck is only "an interesting case," a mere puppet who at command wiggles his ears. Although Büchner as a doctor and scientist was a contributor to the scientific ethos of his age, he was equally aware of science's responsibility to humanity and deeply felt the suffering and distress of his fellowman.

One of the best and most informative examinations of Büchner's style can be found in Helmut Krapp's study,[17] which attempts to analyse and determine the various stylistic devices. The first of these is discontinuity of speech achieved through frequent caesuras, a complete disregard for normal grammatic order, and the breaking up of sentences into a series of words. The isolation of words through a sudden interruption signalled by a dash or frequent repetition indicates a chaotic emotional atmosphere and draws attention to fixed themes independent of strict sequential thought; this suggests the psychological obsession which gradually gains complete control of the passive Woyzeck.

Often the text loses the very character of speech to become interjections of pain and despair. The structure of dialogue and monologue attains a significance beyond that of the realistic or naturalistic literary schools, for the protagonist's psychological state is not the result of the content matter of his speech but rather the consequence of the fragmentary, confused method of presentation. Krapp further singles out three words, "stab," "dance," and "round and round" (one word in German—*immerzu*), which return constantly with the repetitive value of the leitmotif. They become the very stigma of Woyzeck's madness, demonstrating the gradual stripping away of his will and his growing servitude to the "it" as he hears a command to kill Marie.

> WOYZECK: Round and round! Round and round! Stop the music! (Stretches himself out on the ground.) What's that? What are you saying? Louder, louder—stab, stab the bitch wolf dead? Stab, stab the bitch wolf dead! Should I? Must I? Do I hear it here, too? Does the wind say it too? I keep on hearing it, round and round, stab dead, dead!

Direct quotations from well known folk songs, fairy tales, and the Bible are effectively incorporated into the text of the play and become an essential part of the personal expression of each character. The diction of *Woyzeck* goes far beyond any mere copy of the "people's tongue" sought after by the naturalists. Krapp maintains that it anticipates rather expressionism and its concern with the actual form of speech. Stammering utterances, grammatic dislocation, and isolation, the greater intimacy of the Hessian dialect, word motifs, all are elements of everyday language; and the portrayal of such, in part, explains the realistic tendency of the young dramatist.

Franz Mautner, acknowledging his indebtedness to Krapp, is more specifically concerned with style as a revelation of the tragedy's message and states from the very outset of his article "Word Patterns, Meaning Structure, and 'Idea' in Büchner's *Woyzeck*" that the style proves that the play is not a social drama but is concerned essentially with the universal theme of human suffering. In the speech of each individual, the same single words always appear, bearing powerful associations and thematic import. In most scenes a few nouns or adjectives stand out through their strong nature or through repetition; they thus color the whole scene, endowing it with its own individual nature and revealing the meaning of the drama.

Although the single scenes are autonomous in images and action, they remain links in a dramatic whole. Unity of action is maintained since Woyzeck appears in all but two scenes while thematic consistency, created through constantly returning emotional and intellectual word motifs such as "red mouth," "stinks," or "nature" endows the tragedy with an inner continuity. Mautner asserts that key words have three different effects and purposes: characterizing motifs which constitute expressions of personality, thematic motifs that emphasize the basic issues of the drama, and functional motifs which act as structural elements bestowing unity upon the play. "It has been demonstrated that *Woyzeck* is a work of art structured and composed to the very last detail. . . ."[18]

Before delving into actual performances, a brief outline of the so-called "*Woyzeck* problem" is most essential, for the various divergent, often diametrically opposed points of view are in part centered around this hotly debated issue. The very crux of the matter lies in the fragmentary, moldy, barely legible state of the four manuscripts brought to light by Karl Emil Franzos, the first editor of Büchner's complete works. Of the four versions, one consists of only two scenes while the most important copy indicates Büchner's attempt to organize the material according to a uniform plan. Consequently, editors and directors must face the unenviable task of creating a homogeneous, performable whole from four incomplete sources.

In 1967, the first volume of Werner Lehmann's important historical, critical edition appeared, containing his reconstruction of the manuscripts. The sequence of scenes provides a major cause of controversy; but the difficulty hinges on an even more heated dispute, that of the proper conclusion. The tragedy was never finished. The protagonist could meet his end through accidental drowning, the conclusion arbitrarily added by Franzos, or he could surrender to or be captured by the authorities for trial and execution, the fate of the historical Woyzeck. In this instance, the central figure would tend to represent the downtrodden lower class with the result that the play itself would run the risk of being categorized as a social revolutionary drama. It is evident that the "*Woyzeck* problem" has by no means been resolved, and one can only conclude that the work will remain, in the words of Horst Oppel, "literary criticism's child of sorrow."[19]

As a further complication, the scenes completely lack the well organized, successive or climactic development characteristic of the classical model. Aesthetic independence, release from causal categories, and the rejection of the traditional scheme of rising action, climax, and dénouement emphasize the individual value of each dramatic unit, anticipating Brecht's epic theater. This culminates in a summation of theatrical projections thematically complete and efficient in themselves. Since each scene lacks an expressed relationship to the following or its predecessor, the onus of interpretation falls largely upon the director who, from several disparates, must form a unified production.

This procedure is not as arbitrary as it might appear at first glance. Closer examination discloses a conscious effort to build a scene around a scene or in direct contrast to the following, while the effective use of leitmotifs provides an element of structural unity. Also the plot, outstanding in its simplicity and lack of complications and intrigues, follows a persecuted individual to his foreseen fate. Indeed, the action of the play may be summarized in a few words, and in this sense Karl Viëtor has compared it to the street ballad.[20]

Also responsible for a significant public performance of *Danton's Death*, the Germanist Dr. Eugen Kilian successfully premièred *Woyzeck* with the aid of the revolving stage of the Residenztheater, Munich, and the highly suggestive sets designed by Alfred Roller. Immediately, critics noticed how singularly suitable for the theater *Woyzeck* could be under Kilian's careful supervision. As the review of the *Münchener Post* expressed it, "Only on the stage is revealed the complete magic of language of those hurrying sentences which are condensed into a red mist of mood which plunges the whole heaven into flames."[21]

Or, in the assessment of Colin Ross, "On the other hand [i.e., as opposed to the performance of *Danton's Death*], the impression left by *Wozzeck*[22] was completely uniform and deep. A stage fragment, which loving hands carefully put together from pages yellow with age taken from Büchner's literary remains, came to life here for the first time in a fashion which was frighteningly vivid and strangely true to nature. These many short, almost disconnected images, some of which consist of only a single sentence, are in their totality of a devastating tragic effect."[23]

Albert Steinrück who played the title role and later made it one of his most famous, did not prove to be especially memorable, finding it difficult to depict a passive antihero. On the whole, this introduction of Büchner to the German theater was a literary production inspired by Büchner's one hundredth birthday, but surprisingly it heralded both the acceptance of Büchner on the twentieth-century stage and a new understanding for a nonidealistic, nineteenth-century drama.

Viktor Barnowsky directed the first Berlin version in December 1913, together with *Leonce and Lena*. It was generally felt that this interpretation, lasting one and a half hours, was too drawn out and lacked unity. Also, the single décor, a valley surrounded by sharp cliffs devised by Svend Gade in an attempt to provide the complexity of individual scenes with a uniform frame of reference, appeared inappropriate for a passive protagonist. On this occasion, Steinrück as Woyzeck dispensed with the "idealistic pathos"[24] of his Munich performance and adopted a more realistic style of acting which found favor with the critics. "Steinrück was also successful with his Woyzeck in Berlin. His tormented fusilier is not as profound as Büchner saw him, but he is moving in his silence, shocking in his primitiveness, and there were almost great moments when in this solid, stiff actor a modest lyricism came to the surface."[25]

A production directed by Arthur Rundt in the Residenzbühne, Vienna, 1914, again with Steinrück as Woyzeck, led to a typical Viennese phenomenon, a theater scandal. Whereas the *Österreichische Volks-zeitung* called into question the drama's literary merit: "The play is put together from a truly endlessly long row of scenic images which are run off without interruption from eight till ten o'clock until the reel becomes empty. Thank God!"[26] the *Wiener Abendpost* and the *Neues Wiener Tagblatt* came to Büchner's defense, the latter seeing him as a precursor of modern realistic drama.

Barnowsky returned to *Woyzeck* in March 1920, again in the Berlin Lessingtheater. He made few changes from his 1913 reading except to update the play according to expressionistic conventions, and to underline the political content, calling it a social proletarian tragedy. However, there arose a contradiction between naturalistic and expressionistic elements: Cäsar Klein's sets conjured up the unreal, the symbolic to suggest an overwhelming atmospheric intensity, but Eugen Klöpfer, who acted the part of Woyzeck, gave a naturalistic portrayal completely at odds with the more idealistic concept of the role held by Steinrück. Once more the production seemed to drag on and failed to provide a consistent point of view.

These criticisms were to a large extent overcome in Max Reinhardt's interpretation presented in the Deutsche Theater, Berlin, on 5 April 1921. In order to create a closed environment and to accentuate the symbolic level, Heartfield and Dworsky designed a décor whereby the realistically oriented sets were grouped together in the middle of the revolving stage, while a black frame surrounded the field of action. The elimination of long pauses to ensure quick transitions, mood-reinforcing lighting effects, the inclusion of the carnival scene, and the recognition of the importance of gesture and mime constituted some of Reinhardt's innovations. Despite the rapid changes, the drama lasted longer than Barnowsky's version and was called long-winded by some critics, but Reinhardt, anxious to promote *Woyzeck* on its own merit, avoided detracting from the mood by not offering a second play on the same evening. He also side-stepped the pitfall of the politically inspired reading by endeavoring to remain on more neutral ground. In the words of Siegfried Jacobsohn, "But in the realm of aesthetics, the main thing is surely how Reinhardt sings his song in his fashion—to perfection, a rounded, balanced, sweet tone, a *bel canto* which no one else could achieve."[27]

Having played Woyzeck for Reinhardt, Eugen Klöpfer directed his own rendering of the tragedy in October 1921 in which he underscored the fragmentary nature of the work. Since the stage as a whole was never in full view, significant human groupings were given special visual meaning by skillfully utilized spotlights. Part of the acting area always remained in darkness so that the stage hands or actors could set up new props during the performance. This technique, frequently exploited in many subsequent productions, totally eliminated the necessity of the curtain. Writing for the *Wiener Arbeiterzeitung*, Otto König remarked, "Klöpfer's production offers a fine example of how one must play such glowing, uninhibited scenes which haven't been technically understood at all. One wasn't aware of the fragmentary nature."[28] In such an approach, the play runs the risk of losing contact with reality, but this danger was countered by Klöpfer's naturalistic, animalistic portrayal of

Woyzeck which won him the acclaim of the *Neues Wiener Journal*. "This actor has captured the secret of portraying human beings to the last detail."[29] The staging's ecstatic overtones can be explained by the persistent desire to ignore the historic Büchner and to see him theatrically as a forerunner of expressionism and politically as a precursor of Marx.

This politicizing bias continued to predominate in the Mannheim Nationaltheater's production of September 1922, which amounted to a worker's stage version, directed by Eugen Felber. However, the reviewer of the *Mannheimer Generalanzeiger* perceptively recognized how readily *Woyzeck* lends itself to the subjective whim of the director and expressed the opinion that Büchner would have little sympathy with modern social revolutionaries. A staging which opened in May 1925 in Cologne placed considerable stress upon the more universal level while downplaying the proletarian slant. A thoughtful interpretation, it was nonetheless found lacking in emotion and earthiness.

In this same vein, J. Fehling directed a *Woyzeck* in the Schillertheater, Berlin, that the critic Alfred Kerr called "the strongest of the *Woyzeck* productions."[30] Because Fehling sought to avoid all revolutionary tendencies in order to delineate a realistic slice of life, he saw in *Woyzeck* the general human tragedy of a persecuted individual living in a hostile world. Particularly noteworthy was his use of the revolving stage to supply immediate transition from the "Tavern" to the "Open Field" so that the "round and round" rhythm of the dance could be extended without interruption into the nature scene and thus converted into the "stab" motif.

Under the Nazi regime, not an environment especially conducive to Büchner's works, political references or inferences had to be deleted at all cost. However, on the occasion of the one hundredth anniversary of Büchner's death, Peter Stanchina limited himself to the poet Büchner in an overall realistic performance on 1 February 1937 in the Frankfurt Schauspielhaus. The private fate of an individual was interpreted as a universal symbol of human suffering while considerable effort was expended in producing a supporting oppressive atmosphere aided by Caspar Neher's appropriate décor and by Hans Jungbauer's Woyzeck, which Fritz Kraus called "a psychological masterpiece."[31]

When the Freie Volksbühne of the Kurfürstendamm Theater, Berlin, came to England in June of 1957, one of its offerings at Sadler's Wells was *Woyzeck* directed by Oscar Fritz Schuh. Although *Leonce and Lena* found little favor with the British press, *Woyzeck* was somewhat more positively received as a "study in what we should today call the expressionistic style of mental aberration" (*The Times*).[32] Singled out for special praise were Bruno Dallansky's moving interpretation of the title role, Ida Krottendorf's unsentimentalized Marie, Charles Regnier's Doctor, a "psychiatrist who anticipates Freud,"[33] and the proficient treatment of the fragmented scenes in the manner of a "film scenario, each short scene creatin a tension which is slackened or tautened by the next."[34]

A similar staging with almost the identical cast was presented in September 1962 in the newly opened Cologne Schauspielhaus, and it could be said to denote a growing trend towards experimentation which would continue into the seventies. As the reviewer Wolfgang Werth aptly remarked, "[In] the whole of German stage literature, there is no work which permits of so many and so different interpretations."[35] In this particular instance, Schuh fashioned a montage effect by including several scenes from the earlier manuscripts and by even adding interpolations of his own invention. Although this practice met with the disapproval of Werth, "[for] by montage one does not achieve an appropriate synthesis, only a distortion," the performance was nonetheless warmly received by the public.

An English production of *Woyzeck* was sponsored by the Royal Academy of Dramatic Art as part of a special exercise in directing by Richard Franklin. An essentially positive review, appearing in the 8 May 1964 issue of *The Times*, pointed above all to the Brechtian influence: the swift episodic scene changes, the addition of a musical commentary, a symbolic cross complete with Woyzeck's name exhibited before the play began, and a pragmatic treatment which shunned emotional extremes. But Franklin, who astutely designated Büchner as "a revolutionary who didn't believe in revolution," resisted the temptation of a Marxian approach by concentrating on Woyzeck the individual. "One was left finally with mixed emotions of social despair and relief at the completion of a cycle. Mr. Franklin succeeded in turning what was primarily a laboratory experiment into an evening of highly effective theatre."

In April 1966, New York City witnessed a guest performance of *Woyzeck* together with Goethe's *The Accomplices* by the Bavarian State Theater under the direction of Hans Lietzau. Although both dramas were presented in German, transitor radios provided simultaneous translation, an arrangement which seems to have worked out to everyone's satisfaction. Stanley Kauffmann characterized Goethe's comedy as a tedious, poor choice but "[then] we came to Georg Büchner's wonderful work *Woyzeck*. . . . It is a play of silence, with enough understated dialogues to define the quiet interstices that wind through it like pearl-grey filament. It is a *Hamlet* of the low-born."[36] Jürgen Rose contrived a permanent set consisting of the lower section of a grey-brick courtyard which most of the evening remained in almost total gloom and contributed significantly to the oppressive aura.

Kauffmann found fault with Lietzau's rather monotonous treatment of the scenes, all seeming too much alike, and with Elisabeth Orth's interpretation of Marie, who came across more as "a distraught suburban housewife in the middle of the day than a slattern." Since he also refers to her as "a local tart" in his plot summary, it is clear that he failed to grasp Büchner's notion of Marie as an unfortunate victim of sex. However, perhaps Kauffmann's harsh judgment would have been mitigated had he remained till the end of the play. A publishing deadline necessitated his premature departure from the theater.

In November 1967, Cologne was the site of an unusual production furnished by a guest appearance of the Polish Stary Teatr, Cracow. In line with the note of social protest common to all of Büchner's works, the director, Swinarski, concluded the drama with a post-mortem examination conducted by the Doctor. After the latter, with showman-like gestures, sliced open the chest of the drowned Woyzeck lying beside Marie's cadaver, the students boldly gazed into the exposed chest cavity. To counterbalance the political note and to provide a universally valid context, Swinarski transformed the tragedy into a ballad set in the folk-song tradition of Polish Galicia at the beginning of the nineteenth century and underscored the dimension by an imaginative use of leitmotif: at the end of each episode, a rustic votive picture portraying the heart of Christ descended in the place of a curtain and thus supplied a visual representation of both the poignant issues of human suffering and of the general religiosity of the peasant class. "Thanks to Swinarski's conception and thanks to his ensemble, he succeeds in bringing to the stage intellectual theater as living drama" (Helene Schreiber).[37]

"Ingmar Bergman's revolutionary production of Büchner's *Woyzeck* remains the highlight of the Stockholm theatrical season. Aiming at a twofold reform, both social and aesthetic, the production has radically changed the conditions that restricted theatergoing to the well-to-do."[38] In an effort to prevent "the theater from dying out" (Bergman),[39] the famous Swedish director sought to encourage the popularization of *Woyzeck* by means of an arena stage constructed especially for the event in the Royal Dramatic Theater. To win the people back into the playhouse, Bergman extended his campaign not only to the actual performance, but to the preparation as well.

After three weeks during which the company rehearsed in private, the public was invited to attend two daily practice sessions and offer their suggestions. Many, including critics, teachers, and drama students, took advantage of this opportunity to partake of a unique dramatic experience. For example, after some

In an attempt to establish greater rapport between the actors and the audience, Ingmar Bergman—in his production of Woyzeck—had one hundred and fifty seats placed directly on the stage and the upper circle and the gallery were completely eliminated. The resultant theater-in-the-round re-established personal, intimate relationships between actors and audience.

BEATA BERGSTRÖM, STOCKHOLM

discussion with the audience, a general consensus was reached to forego the realistic detail of blood upon Woyzeck because this would lessen audience participation by reducing the appeal to the imagination. When *Woyzeck* was deemed ready after three weeks of open rehearsal, it was played twice nightly. In order to break down any remaining vestige of class structure, only one uniform price of admission was charged, and seats were unnumbered.

Also Bergman successfully placed the tragedy into a Swedish fin-de-siècle context to which the audience could relate more readily: gray Swedish uniforms, an effective use of local dialects, or a horse which defecated cotton-wool balls in the Swedish national colors. A pseudo-chorus seated on either side of the arena reproduced the noise and commotion of the crowd scenes in the tavern, barracks, or fairgrounds. All the actors seemed to be well cast in their respective roles, but Tommy Berggren's portrayal of a schizophrenic Woyzeck proved particularly commendable. "The growth of the actors' art in a shared experience with their director and one another, as well as a living audience disposed to be affected or otherwise enthralled by the creative process, is happily on record."[40]

Writing for *The Times* 9 July 1969, Henry Raynor endeavored to place Büchner in a specific literary context: "Büchner's *Woyzeck* is the first triumph of naturalistic theater" and then proceeded to apply this yardstick to a very modern approach. "La Mama—Plexus II, who offer [*Woyzeck*] as the second play in their season [1969] at the Arts Theatre, do not see [it] in this way. They enter the stage under a narrow white curtain and involve themselves in a cleverly choreographed, grotesque chaos of movement to a painful, sustained electronic noise before a word is spoken. Naturalism is entirely abandoned."[41] Although Büchner's final drama does display obvious affinities with naturalism, its revolutionary language and structure burst asunder the confining limits of any literary tag and hence justify some of the more radical experiments of more recent years.

This production aimed at presenting a generally depressing view of a world gone mad, while opting to ignore the social or political undercurrent. Consequently, costumes failed to differentiate between privates and officers, and emphasis was placed upon the "athletic elegance" with which the company moved about the stage, often to the detriment of the spoken word. "They do not, it seems, misunderstand the play; they simply make use of it for their own pessimistic ends."

The year 1969 also proved to be equally prolific in experimentation with the *Woyzeck* fragments upon German-speaking stages. No less than six major productions can be documented, but perhaps the most radical was that offered at the twenty-third Ruhr Festival in Recklinghausen. Willi Schmidt mystified audiences and inspired generally negative reviews with his montage interpretation of *Leonce and Lena* and *Woyzeck*. Referring to one of Büchner's letters in which he wrote that he was in the process of "letting some people kill themselves or get married on paper," Schmidt saw in these two plays "dramatic types of despair"[42] which could conceivably support and enhance one another in a combined effort.

The first scene of *Leonce and Lena* was immediately followed by an abridged version of the scene where Woyzeck describes his hallucinatory vision. A procedure of juxtaposing a group of scenes from the comedy with a selection from the tragedy continued almost four hours until both conclusions were played simultaneously to suggest a merging of one drama into the other. This partial destruction of the texts was supposed to demonstrate in a transparent fashion the parallels between the two works. To suggest these correspondences, Peter Brogle played both Woyzeck and Leonce, Hans Clarin supported him as Andres and Valerio, while Eva Kotthaus acted the part of Marie and Rosetta.

Many objections were raised against this produc-

DOCTOR: I saw it, Woyzeck; you pissed on the street, pissed on the wall, like a dog. And to think you get two cents a day. Woyzeck, that's bad. The world is getting bad, very bad.

In a production directed by Niels-Peter Rudolf for the Deutsche Schauspielhaus in Hamburg in April 1970, Fritz Lichtenhahn portrayed the persecuted man in his animal simplicity against a bright empty stage.

VOLKER CANARIS, COLOGNE

tion, among others the inappropriateness of casting Peter Brogle in his double role, the unsuitability of Schmidt's self-designed, merry-go-round-like structure for the depressing atmosphere of *Woyzeck*, and the priority of aesthetic effects at the expense of suspense and inner unity. "The bright ideas and the gags which often came across artificially could not save the play. Much remained isolated in space. The great correlation was not achieved. One missed the expected contrasts just as much as their neutralization in a new unity. Too bad" (Hans Schwab-Felisch).[43]

As if in answer to Raynor's review of La Mama-

Plexus II interpretation of 1969, the Yale Repertory staged *Woyzeck* in April 1971 in the naturalistic mode. "Somehow, one hopes for fever and hallucinating on the part of the director, Tom Haas. . . . Instead, the production accents the naturalistic side of the work" (Mel Gussow).[44] This version again pointed out the danger inherent in stressing one aspect of an extremely rich drama. It dragged on, becoming a tedious exercise for the viewer, an impression reinforced by the uniformity of the acting. "Taking this production at surface value, one might think the play was a melodramatic libretto about a crazy, jealous barber who murders his mistress."[45]

A highly unusual approach to *Woyzeck* was adopted by the Teatro Stabile in Turin, inspired by the literary critic Giorgio Zampa. Like Brecht who disapproved of the various attempts to complete the play, Zampa insisted that the fragmentary form constituted a "productive hindrance."[46] He rejected all previous stagings and recommended limitation to the four variants outlined by Werner Lehmann in the first volume of his critical edition (1967). Director Virginio Puecher thus presented the four readings as an experiment in open form which he entitled "The Unfinished Drama of *Woyzeck*." The repetition of scenes in slightly altered form helped to underline the historic background as well as to depict a vision of man victimized by cruel indifferent forces.

Whereas the first version was performed at breathtaking speed with all the actors continually present on stage, forming constantly changing human configurations, the final reading, being more fully developed by Büchner, demanded a well-balanced slower tempo. Klaus Völker preferred the first energetic rendition

BARKER: Show your talent! Show your bestial reasonableness. Put human society to shame! Gentlemen, this animal which you see before you, a tail on his body, standing on his four hoofs, is a member of all learned societies, is a professor of our university where the students learn to ride and fight from him.

Puecher's novel production of *Woyzeck* for the Teatro Stabile, Turin (1970–71) made extensive use of lighting effects against curtains or an austere, wooden-plank wall. Here Roberto Pistone extols the beast at the expense of human dignity.

TEATRO STABILE DI TORINO

because "the scenes which consist of only one sentence receive a sharply defined form which corresponds to Büchner's written copy and which asks the question about the nature and power of those social conditions which lead to destruction" while the final effort tended to fall "into illusionary genre painting and exaggerated rhetoric."

Critics and directors alike have long recognized that *Woyzeck* represents one of the most difficult plays to stage successfully. Perhaps this was demonstrated most emphatically in February 1972 when Friedrich Dürrenmatt produced Büchner's incomplete drama for the Zürich Schauspielhaus. Following the example of many of his predecessors, Dürrenmatt devised his own montage of twenty-five scenes after an analysis of the variants. His interpretation, beginning with the "Open Field" hallucination performed on a totally empty stage, seemed to culminate in a scene lifted from the first manuscript, which depicts a barber shaving a noncommissioned officer. Assuming that Woyzeck is synonymous with the barber and the Drum Major with the noncommissioned officer, Dürrenmatt used this episode to accentuate and concentrate the sense of rivalry and hatred between the two men, which reaches a climax as the Drum Major forces the defeated and humiliated barber to drink the shaving water.

In the light of this male contest, all other motivation behind Woyzeck's homicide became of secondary importance. Most reviewers had serious reservations concerning this conception while pointing to numerous other weaknesses such as the miscasting of Christiane Hörbiger as Marie, a much too slow dramatic movement, the lack of a unifying principle to link the individual scenes, and the reduction of the caricatural portraits of the Captain and the Doctor to innocuous characterizations. In his assessment for the *National-Zeitung*, Basel, Hugo Leber remarked, "How does Woyzeck respond to the Captain's question about the weather? 'Bad, Captain, bad.' "[47]

In December 1972, Die Brücke, a special company from West Germany, which in a five-month period visited fifty-one cities in southeastern Asia, Australia, and North America, offered as the high point of its tour a fourteen-day guest performance of *Woyzeck* in the Barbizon Plaza Theater, New York City. The actors spoke German, but the program notes were provided in English. Very simple permanent sets were efficiently utilized, one unit always being illuminated while properties were moved into another blacked-out area by the players themselves. This suggested a sense of rapid, inexorable forward motion which complemented the excellent acting of the cast. Elisabeth Endriss as Marie managed to combine convincingly sensuality and sincere remorse, which elicited some sympathy from the audience. A sensitive review by A. H. Weiler concluded: "We may be removed in time from Büchner's kaleidoscope of vintage drama, but its inherent meanings seem timeless, occasionally moving and, as a whole, strangely disturbing."[48]

The stage of the Open Space became the center of theatrical attention in London in February 1973. Charles Marowitz, a director notorious for his Shakespeare cutups, presented an experimental version of *Woyzeck* as part of his plan to reinterpret classical dramas on the basis of modern experience. Going back to the historical court case (the performance began with the reading of the death sentence), Marowitz changed the tragedy into a trial, in which each member of the cast eventually arrived at his or her verdict.

With total irreverence the traditional sequence was cast aside (the black fairy tale was the second scene), actors were given more than one role (the Drum Major also acted the part of the Jew while Woyzeck doubled as the monkey and the horse), and surprising stage effects were developed to startle the audience. (When the Drum Major straddled Marie, the rhythm of Woyzeck's accelerating march accompanied their sexual union.) Woyzeck, interpreted by David Schofield, was depicted as "the eternal human animal,"[49] the state to which each of us could conceivably be reduced if the thin veneer of culture were stripped away.

The growing importance of *Woyzeck* for the American stage can be readily ascertained in two New York City productions, one in April 1975 by the Classic Stage Company and another in March 1976 by the Shaliko Company, both reviewed by Clive Barnes of the *New York Times*. On the whole, the former's treatment elicited a favorable reaction from Barnes who sees in *Woyzeck* "the first great modern tragedy."[50] "It is virtually impossible to think of *Woyzeck* as anything but a play of our century."[51] Director Christoph Martin concentrated on smooth, effortless scenic transition with a realistic emphasis. Most of the acting, adequately done, took place behind a low fence which shut off the middle of the stage. When not speaking their lines, the players, dressed in generally dismal costumes, would retire outside of the dark fence to observe the protagonist. "This is a fascinating *Woyzeck* and a good theatrical introduction to a play only too rare."[52]

In contrast, the Shaliko Company's version "appeared crude, emblematic and undramatic"[53] largely as a result of the heavy-handed acting of the cast. The one exception proved to be the excellent performance of Joseph Chaikin as Woyzeck. "With bright raising eyes stuck in a gray potato face, with his voice reduced to an oppressed monotone and his gestures imprisoned to the futility almost of grimace, Mr. Chaikin wandered through the play as if subconsciously in search of a better cast."[54]

In the 1970s, *Woyzeck* continues to be the object of what has been called an "emancipating trend,"[55] somewhat arbitrary interpretations often seeking novelty solely for the sake of novelty. The combined city companies of Krefeld-Mönchengladbach, Germany, co-ordinated a mammoth *Woyzeck-Wozzeck* production of Büchner and Berg in 1972. A Munich version of the same year commenced with the market scene and concluded with the departure of a hearse bearing away Marie's body as the Grandmother and the children silently observed the proceedings. In Frankfurt, an attempt was made to create a play in a play; the curtain was raised upon an annual fair, a frame action in the context of which a wandering troupe entertained the crowd with a *Woyzeck* performance.

Peter Borchardt's 1973 staging in Ulm achieved considerable effect from a giant grey megaphone constructed on the stage from within which Woyzeck expressed his despair of the world while Christof Nel disconcerted a Bremen audience in February 1974 with a strange combination of surrealism (the Captain-Doctor street confrontation was played on stilts!) and ultra-realism (in the pond scene, Woyzeck splashed around in real water, looking for the knife). In March 1975 the newly renovated Hannover Schauspielhaus was opened with Büchner's *Woyzeck* introduced by a prologue, a one-act play by Gerhard Kelling called "The Soundness of Mind of the Murderer Johann Christian Woyzeck," a circus routine enacted by a caged Woyzeck under the supervision of the historical Professor Clarus.

One year later, Alfred Kirchner and the Staatstheater, Stuttgart, in a manner reminiscent of Puecher's Turin experiment, presented in one evening two

Woyzecks, the first, based upon the earliest manuscript, entitled "I smell, I smell blood," and the second,
a sequence of scenes from the last two versions, called
"We poor people."[56] As Georg Hensel said, in his
review of Peter Palitzsch's Frankfurt interpretation of
August 1976, in which Woyzeck returned to the pond
and parodistically climbed up a ladder to touch the
stage moon, "A book could be written about the
different Woyzeck versions."[57]

Finally, as a fitting monument to the amazing
adaptability of Büchner's short masterpiece, mention
should be made of a production by La Compagnie du
Centre National des Arts, Ottawa, in October 1976.
First presented in the Canadian capital in 1974 and in
Montreal in 1975, it won the praise of critics and audiences alike. The two codirectors, Jean Herbiet and
Felix Mirbt, took advantage of marionettes, puppeteers, and actors to illustrate "the manipulation of
human beings through the exercise of power."[58]
Normally one might expect such a collaboration to be
detrimental to a work intended exclusively for actors,
but in this instance it appeared singularly appropriate
and in keeping with a favorite image of Büchner who
wrote in *Danton's Death*, "We are puppets drawn on a
string; we ourselves are nothing, nothing."

The staging of the Centre National des Arts gave a
literal interpretation of this image, a dramatized meta-
phor. Essentially there were three levels of action.
First of all, attention was drawn to the marionettes
who represented the protagonists of the play and in
whose "sculptured features the entire character"[59]
was symbolically portrayed. Then there were the five
puppeteers who manipulated the figures on stage and
achieved a monumental effect when they reflected

Büchner was especially enamored of the puppet image which the Ottawa production of La Compagnie du Centre National des Arts exploited effectively. In *Leonce and Lena* Valerio refers to the masked titular characters in the following terms: "Ladies and gentlemen, look at these two people, one of each sex, a little man and a little woman, a gentleman and a lady! Nothing but art and mechanism, nothing but pasteboard and watch-springs . . . . These persons are so perfectly built that you couldn't distinguish them from other people if you didn't know that they are only pasteboard; you could make them into members of human society."

NATIONAL ARTS CENTRE, OTTAWA

through mime the reactions of their charges. In the words of Wolf Wetkens of *The Financial Times*, London, England, "What made [the] staging haunting were those few moments when the emotion of the marionette spread to the manipulator holding its strings and those when the puppeteer tried to comfort his creature."[60] On the third level a group of six actors and actresses attired in aristocratic courtly costumes, occupied a sort of royal box overlooking the stage from which they both spoke the lines of the play and served as an ideal audience.

"The characters are puppets manipulated by soldiers who are putting on a show for the officers and ladies seated above the set—facing the audience. Yet the lines dividing audience and actors are often blurred: the words are spoken by the aristocrats from their luxurious theater box, the actors on the stage are implicated in the dramatic action on a level other than that of the puppeteers, while the puppets themselves advise, admonish, and at one point attack the manipulators" (Jeff Lewis).[61] Wherever this staging has gone, it has met with enthusiastic reviews. "*Woyzeck* . . . is a highly original, multi-faceted, and totally spellbinding theatre experience . . . for the elements which combine to make this such a unique production are seldom united in such exquisitely balanced proportions" (Myron Galloway).[62]

6. CONCLUSION:
THE BÜCHNER PHENOMENON

The German dramatist Carl Zuckmayer once remarked in reference to his own works, "I really didn't
have any models unless one wants to name that great
model of all modern theater . . . Georg Büchner."[1]
The most obvious testimony to Büchner's grasp or
intuitive understanding of the archetypal essence of
drama has been the continued influence his relatively
meager example has had upon the development of the
European stage from the end of the nineteenth century to the present. In the late 1880s, the most successful German playwright of naturalism, Gerhard
Hauptmann, gave a lecture to a literary association in
Berlin in which he promoted Büchner's works as
good examples in a naturalistic vein.

Hauptmann saw in *Woyzeck* the first passive, proletarian hero determined by heredity and environment. The dignity of tragedy which Büchner be-
stowed upon the common man can also be detected in
Hannele (1839), *Henschel the Carter* (1898), but
especially in *The Weavers* (1892) where Hauptmann's compassionate concern for suffering humanity
and his ability to empathize with the basically inarticu-

late members of the lower class resulted in a master-piece.

The caricatures in *Woyzeck* by which Büchner sought to attack hypocritical bourgeois conventions proved a source of inspiration for Frank Wedekind's *Spring's Awakening* (1891), a pre-expressionistic drama protesting against the lack of sex education among the young. The representatives of the middle-class establishment are portrayed as perverted, grotesque individuals in the tradition of the Captain or the Doctor. Also the instinctual female characters, such as the prostitute Marion (*Danton's Death*) or Marie (*Woyzeck*), contributed to Wedekind's glorification of "the true animal, the beautiful, wild animal"[2] as exemplified in the amoral Lulu (*Earth Spirit*, 1895 and *Pandora's Box*, 1903).

As previously noted, Büchner's dramas received their first public airing and acceptance in the expressionistic stage style. This group was strongly attracted to Büchner's novel use of language and sensed within it a simplicity and primordial strength which they strove to emulate. The expressionists also broke with tradition in their rejection of the well-made play, preferring instead a series of individual projections, each complete in itself and representing a station of inner development rather than a scene of dramatic progress (cf. Hasenclever's *Humanity*, 1918 or Toller's *Hinke-mann*, 1923). Büchner again showed the way.

Woyzeck is undoubtedly best known in America in the operatic adaptation composed by Alban Berg. Music from Bach through Beethoven to Brahms and Bruckner has been predominantly tonal, dissonance being ultimately resolved with consonance. A student of Arnold Schoenberg and a convert to his twelve-tone system, Berg was determined to set *Woyzeck* to music after he witnessed a performance in 1914 and recognized it as a dissonant, atonal drama. In order to avoid the very real danger of fragmentation, he decided to divide the play into three acts of five scenes, each of which was constructed according to a definite musical form such as a march, sonata, or a rhapsody. Most critics now see in Berg's opera an extremely successful marriage of music and drama, the former serving to intensify the tragic impact of the latter. For example, the grotesque and sadistic personality of the Captain is unforgettably captured in his cruel, arhythmical laugh.

Wozzeck makes extreme demands upon the singers, requiring a scope of vocal expressions ranging from ordinary discourse and sung speech to normal singing. When the work was premièred on 14 December 1925 under the baton of Erich Kleiber, it created a sensational scandal and journalistic uproar, but with the passage of time, it has increased in popularity and ironically may now be considered one of the classics of the operatic stage.

By far one of the most-produced German dramatists of the twentieth century has been Bertolt Brecht, who on several occasions stated that he considered Büchner the main source of inspiration in his own literary development. Indeed, just before his death in 1956, he is reported to have told Arthur Adamov that *Woyzeck* heralded the beginning of modern theater. In Büchner, Brecht rightly or wrongly saw a fellow political revolutionary with a strong humanitarian orientation, the creator of a new vital poetic language with a realistic as well as surrealistic flavor and an iconoclast of the stage who broke with the stereotyped traditions of the German drama. Brecht's epic theater, which replaced the linear plot with independent self-sufficient scenes, may have been partially derived from Büchner's example. This influence extends far beyond stylistic and structural considerations to include even thematic preoccupations, for Galy Gay, the passive antihero of *Man Is Man* (1926) follows in the footsteps of Woyzeck, as he does not act but is rather acted upon.

As a further manifestation of the power of attraction exerted by Büchner's work, the Salzburg Festival hosted the first performance of an operatic interpretation of *Danton's Death* by Gottfried von Einem in 1947. One half of the score was written down before the end of World War II and hence reflects the experiences of the composer under the Nazi regime. With the collaboration of Boris Blacher, von Einem wrote a text consisting of seventeen scenes complemented by six Caspar Neher sets. The music and the staging tend to concentrate attention upon the crowd represented by a chorus. Danton is consequently depicted as a helpless victim surrendered up to a cruel inexorable fate, the incalculable masses, over which he has no control.

Musically von Einem strengthened this impression by stressing the function of the chorus strongly seconded by the orchestra while the solo voices by comparison appear isolated and ineffective. Although this opera has received some support and acclaim, to date it has failed to achieve the popularity enjoyed by Berg's *Wozzeck*.

Arthur Adamov, one of the main proponents of absurd theater, commented, "Between Shakespeare and Molière's *Don Juan* up until Brecht there is nothing except Büchner,"[3] while Eugène Ionesco listed Büchner among the few writers, including Aeschylus, Sophocles, Shakespeare, and Kleist, whom he deemed readable. The members of the French avant-garde discovered in the author of *Leonce and Lena* the poet of existential fear and absurdity. One of the major preoccupations of this modern theater has been the failure of language to provide meaningful communication since it is composed of empty clichés. Not unlike the figures in Büchner's plays, characters tend to speak in a void and are persecuted by an overwhelming sense of ennui conditioned by a terrifying awareness of the irrationality of life. This state of mind frequently leads to an identity crisis similar to that undergone by both Leonce and the imbecile King Peter. Hence, Büchner's influence has been alluded to in Adamov's *The Parody* (1947), Ionesco's *The Bald Soprano* (1948), and Beckett's *Waiting for Godot* (1952).

In more recent times, the pendulum has perhaps begun to swing away from increased abstraction towards historical realism best represented by the documentary plays of Peter Weiss. Many critics have pointed to the obvious parallel between *The Persecution and Assassination of Marat as Performed by the Inmates of the Asylum of Charenton under the Direction of the Marquis de Sade* (1964) and *Danton's Death*, while *Trotzki in Exile* (1971) has been referred to as "the *Danton's Death* of the Russian Revolution" (Ronald Hauser).[4] If the first seventy years of the twentieth century are any clear indication, George Büchner's works will continue to provide a stimulus, a challenge, and a provocation to the directors and dramatists of the future.

NOTES

1. The Life and Times of George Büchner

1. All translations from Büchner are my own and are based upon Werner R. Lehmann's edition: *Sämtliche Werke und Briefe* (Complete Works and Letters), Hamburg: Christian Wegner Verlag, Vol. I, 1967, Vol. II, 1971, or *George Büchner, Werke und Briefe*, ed. Fritz Bergemann, Munich: Deutscher Taschenbuch Verlag, 1975.

2. This quotation attributed to Büchner is drawn from August Becker's court statement (1835/36). See *Georg Büchner. Werke und Briefe*, p. 229.

3. Quoted in *Heritage of Western Civilization*, Vol. II, eds. John Louis Beatley and Oliver A. Johnson, New Jersay: Prentice Hall, 1971, p. 151.

4. Cf. August Becker's court statement, op. cit., p. 307.

2. Büchner's View of Art: *Lenz*

1. Johann Gottfried Herder, *Fragmente über die neuere deutsche Literatur*, 1767/68, and *Von deutscher Art und Kunst*, 1773.

3. *Danton's Death*

1. Lord Byron, "Don Juan," canto I, verse 194.

2. *Der Tag*, 7 January 1902. All translations from German (or French) are my own.

3. Edgar Steiger, *Das Literarische Echo*, 16th Year, book 5, 1 December 1913.

4. From *Vorwärts*, quoted in Ingeborg Strudthoff, *Die Rezeption Georg Büchners durch das deutsche Theater*, Berlin-Dahlem: Colloquium Verlag, 1957, p. 55.

5. Quoted from Gielen's prompt book, Strudthoff, p. 102.

6. *Deutsche Allgemeine Zeitung*, 2 September 1929.

7. *New York Times*, 3 November 1938. All immediately following quotations are to be found in this review.

8. *Daily Worker*, 20 October 1938.

9. *Berliner Illustrierte Nachtausgabe*, 11 December 1939.

10. *Darmstädter Echo*, 20 September 1957.

11. W. Falke, "Tragödie einer Revolution" (Tragedy of a Revolution). Part of the program notes offered by the Detmolder Landestheater. Quoted in Wolfram Viehweg, *Georg Büchners 'Dantons Tod' auf dem deutschen Theater* (Georg Büchner's Danton's Death in the German Theater), Munich: Laokoon-Verlag, 1964, p. 304.

12. *Die Welt*, 7 May 1956.

13. Viehweg, p. 350.

14. *The Times* (London), 28 January 1959. The immediately following quotation is also cited from this review.

15. *Stuttgarter Zeitung*, 6 July 1962. All immediately following quotations are drawn from this article.

16. *Die Welt*, 13 February 1963.

17. *New York Times*, 14 October 1965.

18. Howard Taubman, *New York Times*, 22 October 1965.

19. Ibid.

20. *The Times*, 29 November 1965.

21. Ibid.

22. Quoted in *Die Welt*, Bühnenspiegel, 31 October 1975.

23. Gert Kalow, *Frankfurter Allgemeine Zeitung*, 3 October 1969.

24. Hans Fröhlich, *Stuttgarter Nachrichten*, 1 October 1969.

25. As quoted in a review by Georg Hensel for the *Süddeutsche Zeitung*, 1 October 1969.

26. Georg Hensel, *Süddeutsche Zeitung*, 1 October 1969.

27. *Frankfurter Allgemeine Zeitung*, 3 October 1969.

28. *Frankfurter Allgemeine Zeitung*, 19 January 1970.

29. *The Times*, 4 August 1971.

30. *The Times*, 13 December 1971.

31. Quoted in *The Times*, 13 December 1971.

32. Elke Lehmann-Brauns, *Frankfurter Allgemeine Zeitung*, 3 December 1971.

33. Ibid.

34. *Der Tagesspiegel*, 10 October 1972.

35. *Die Zeit*, 19 November 1976.

4. *Leonce and Lena*

1. Shakespeare, *Hamlet*, Act IV, scene v, lines 175–190.

2. *Jahrhundertwende* (At the Turn of the Century), Danzig, 1936, p. 149.

3. *Neue freie Presse*, 31 December 1911.

4. *Hamburger Fremdenblatt*, 30 January 1912.

5. *Schaubühne*, IX, Heft 52, 1913, p. 1279.

6. Cf. Strudthoff, *Rezeption*, p. 76.

7. *Hamburger Anzeiger*, 7 September 1925.

8. *Völkischer Beobachter*, 25 February 1934.

9. *The Times*, 18 June 1957. All subsequent quotations relating to this production originate with this review.

10. Quoted in *The Times*, 20 April 1959.

11. *The Times*, 20 April 1959.

12. Ibid.

13. *Stuttgarter Nachrichten*, 20 June 1961.

14. *Rheinischer Merkur*, 17 May 1963.

15. Ibid.

16. *Marbacher Zeitung*, 27 July 1968.

17. *Süddeutsche Zeitung*, 9 October 1968.

18. My translation of the program notes. Vienna: Volkstheater, 1969.

19. *The Times*, 1 September 1971.

20. Ibid.

21. *New York Times*, 24 March 1974.

22. *Stuttgarter Nachrichten*, 19 May 1973.

23. Gert Kalow, *Frankfurter Allgemeine Zeitung*, 5 June 1973. All subsequent quotations relating to this production will be drawn from this article.

24. *Die Presse*, 7/8 August 1976.

25. Joachim Kaiser, *Süddeutsche Zeitung*, 14/15 August 1975.

26. Winfried Wild, *Schwäbische Zeitung*, 14 August 1975. All subsequent quotations describing the Schaaf production are drawn from this review.

27. *Badische Neueste Nachrichten*, 7 November 1975.

28. Ibid.

29. Ibid.

30. *Die Welt*, 8 November 1975.

5. *Woyzeck*

1. Robert Mülher, "Georg Büchner und die Mythologie des Nihilismus," in: *Dichtung der Krise* (Wien: Verlag Herold, 1957), p. 99.

2. Georg Büchner, *Politik, Dichtung, Wissenschaft* (Berne: A Franke Verlag, 1949), pp. 189–212.

3. *Dantons Tod and Woyzeck*. Edition with introduction and notes (Manchester, 1954), pp. xix–xxvi.

4. "Georg Büchner. Die Tragödie des Nihilismus" (The Tragedy of Nihilism), in: *Die deutsche Tragödie von Lessing bis Hebbel*, (Hamburg: Hoffmann & Campe, 1961), pp. 513–534.

5. *Re-Interpretations* (London: Thomas & Hudson, 1964), pp. 78–155.

6. Ibid., p. 86.

7. Ibid., p. 104.

8. *Georg Büchner und seine Zeit* (Berlin: Volk und Welt, 1947), pp. 327–335.

9. *Deutsche Realisten des 19. Jahrhunderts* (Berlin: Aufbau Verlag, 1952), p. 66.

10. Ibid., p. 71.

11. Georg Büchner. *Revolutionär und Pessimist* (Georg Büchner. Revolutionary and Pessimist) (Nuremberg: Hans Carl, 1948), p. ix.

12. *Sämtliche Werke* (Complete Works), Vol. 10, "Das Geheimnis des Opfers" (Stuttgart-Bad Canstatt: Fromm, 1960), p. 41.

13. Franz Mautner, "Wortgewebe, Sinnegefüge und 'Idee' in Büchners *Woyzeck*" (Word Patterns, Meaning Structure and 'Idea' in Büchner's *Woyzeck*), in: *Deutsche Vierteljahrsschrift für Literaturwissenschaft und Geistesgeschichte*, 35 (1961), 542–547.

14. Viëtor, pp. 204–205.

15. "Zur Karikatur in der Dichtung Büchners," *Germanisch-Romanische Monatsschrift*, N.F. 8 (1958), 64–71.

16. Viëtor, pp. 196–197.

17. *Der Dialog bei Georg Büchner* (Darmstadt: Gentner, 1958).

18. Mautner, p. 554.

19. *Die tragische Dichtung Georg Büchners* (The Tragic Works of Georg Büchner) (Stuttgart: Hempe, 1951), p. 42.

20. Viëtor, p. 208.

21. *Münchener Post*, 11 November 1913.

22. When Franzos transcribed Büchner's handwriting for his 1879 edition, he mistakenly deciphered "Woyzeck" as "Wozzeck." Since this first complete work represented the standard until the 1920's, critics, directors, and the composer Alban Berg quite consistently used this incorrect spelling.

23. *Zeit im Bild*, 11th Year, No. 48, 26 November 1913.

24. Strudthoff, *Rezeption*, p. 46.

25. Herbert Ihering, *Die Schaubühne*, 9th Year, book 52, 1913, p. 1279.

26. Quoted in Strudthoff, p. 49.

27. From *Das Jahr der Bühne*, vol. 10, 1920/21, p. 134 f.

28. *Wiener Arbeiterzeitung*, 15 May 1921.

29. Quoted in Strudthoff, p. 71.

30. *Berliner Tageblatt*, 15 December 1927.

31. *Frankfurter Zeitung*, 2 February 1923.

32. *The Times*, 18 June 1957.

33. Ibid.

34. Ibid.

35. *Deutsche Zeitung*, 12 September 1962.

36. *New York Times*, 6 April 1966.

37. *Rheinischer Merkur*, 3 November 1967.

38. *The Times*, 2 June 1969.

39. Quoted in *The Times*, 5 February 1969.

40. *The Times*, 2 June 1969.

41. *The Times*, 9 July 1969. All quotations referring to this staging are drawn from this article.

42. Johannes Jacobi, *Die Zeit*, 16 May 1969.

43. *Frankfurter Allgemeine Zeitung*, 9 May 1969.

44. *New York Times*, 15 April 1971.

45. Ibid.

46. Klaus Völker, *Frankfurter Rundschau*, 6 March 1971. All quotations relating to this production are cited from this review.

47. *National-Zeitung*, Basel, 21 February 1972.

48. *New York Times*, 6 December 1972.

49. *The Times*, 20 February 1973.

50. *New York Times*, 25 March 1976.

51. *New York Times*, 13 April 1975.

52. Ibid.

53. *New York Times*, 25 March 1976.

54. Ibid.

55. Dietmar N. Schmidt, *Frankfurter Rundschau*, 11 November 1972.

56. Cf. Wolfgang Ignée, *Stuttgarter Zeitung*, 20 March 1976.

57. *Frankfurter Allgemeine Zeitung*, 30 August 1976.

58. Quoted from a National Arts Centre announcement, 27 September 1976.

59. Myron Galloway, *Montreal Star*, 13 March 1975.

60. *The Financial Times*, May 1974.

61. *The Ottawa Citizen*, 16 April 1974.

62. *Montreal Star*, 13 March 1975.

6. Conclusion: The Büchner Phenomenon

1. Quoted in Horst Bienek, *Werkstattgespräche mit Schriftstellern* (Workshop Conversations with Writers) (Munich: Deutscher Taschenbuch Verlag, 1965), p. 213.

2. Quoted in H. A. and E. Frenzel, *Daten deutscher Dichtung* (German Literature Dates), Vol. II (Munich: Deutscher Taschenbuch Verlag, 1964), p. 135.

3. Quoted in Maurice B. Benn, *The Drama of Revolt* (Cambridge, London, New York, Melbourne: Cambridge University Press, 1976), p. 183.

4. Georg Büchner (New York: Twayne Publishers, 1974), p. 138.

BIBLIOGRAPHY

1. Works by Büchner

Sämtliche Werke und Briefe. Historisch-kritische Ausgabe mit Kommentar, ed. Werner R. Lehmann. Hamburg: Christian Wegner Verlag, Vol. I, 1967.

TRANSLATIONS

The Plays of Georg Büchner. Transl. by Geoffrey Dunlop. London: Gerald Howe, 1927. Also New York: Viking Press, 1928; I. Ravin, 1952; and London: Vision Press, 1952; vol. II, 1971 (cont.).

A Play in Four Acts: "Danton's Death," by Georg Büchner. Transl. by Stephen Spender and Goronwy Rees. London: Faber & Faber, 1939.

Danton's Death. Transl. by Spender and Rees. In *From the Modern Repertoire*, ed. E. R. Bentley. Denver: University of Denver Press, 1949. Ser. I, pp. 29–86.

Woyzeck. Transl. by Henry Schnitzler and Seth Ulman. *New Directions in Prose and Poetry*, no. 12. London: Peter Owen, and New York: Meridian Books, 1950.

Danton's Death. Transl. by Spender and Rees. *Treasury of the Theatre*, ed. J. Gassner, Vol. I. New York: Simon & Schuster, 1951.

Lenz. Transl. by Michael Hamburger. *Partisan Review*, 22 (1955), 31–46, 135–144.

Woyzeck. Transl. by Theodore Hoffmann. *The Modern Theatre*, ed. E. R. Bentley, vol. I. Garden City, N.Y.: Doubleday, 1955.

Danton's Death. Transl. by John Holmstrom. *The Modern Theatre*, ed. E. R. Bentley, vol. V. Garden City, N.Y.: Doubleday, 1957.

Danton's Death. Transl. and adapted by James Maxwell. San Francisco: Chandler Publishing Co., 1961.

Woyzeck and *Leonce and Lena.* Transl. by Carl R. Mueller. San Francisco: Chandler Publishing Co., 1962.

Complete Plays and Prose. Trans. by Carl R. Mueller. New York: Hill and Wang, 1963. Also London: Mac-Gibbon & Kee, 1963.

Danton's Death. Transl. by Theodore H. Lustig. *Classical German Drama.* New York: Bantam Books, 1963.

Woyzeck. Transl. by John Holmstrom. *Three German Plays.* Harmondsworth, Middlesex: Penguin Books, 1963.

Woyzeck. Transl. by Henry J. Schmidt. New York: Bard Books, 1969.

The Plays of Georg Büchner. Transl. by Victor Price. London: Oxford University Press, 1971.

Leonce and Lena—Lenz—Woyzeck. Transl. by Michael Hamburger. Chicago and London: University of Chicago Press, 1972.

2. Secondary Literature

IN GERMAN

Baumann, Gerhart. *Georg Büchner. Die dramatische Ausdruckswelt.* Göttingen: Vandenhoeck & Ruprecht, 1961.

Büttner, Ludwig. *Georg Büchner, Revolutionär und Pessimist.* Nuremberg: Verlag Hans Carl, 1948.

Krapp, Helmut. *Der Dialog bei Georg Büchner.* Darmstadt: Gentner, 1958.

Martens, Wolfgang. "Zur Karikatur in der Dichtung Büchners," *Germanisch-Romanische Monatsschrift*, N.F. 8, 1958.

———— (ed.). *Georg Büchner.* Darmstadt: Wissenschaftliche Buchgesellschaft, 1965. [An excellent collection of essays by critics such as Georg Lukács or Franz Mautner.]

Mayer, Hans. *Georg Büchner und seine Zeit*. Wiesbaden: Limes Verlag, 1946 and 1960; Berlin: Verlag Volk und Welt, 1947, and Aufbau Verlag, 1960.

Oppel, Horst. *Die tragische Dichtung Georg Büchners*. Stuttgart: Hempe, 1951.

Strudthoff, Ingeborg. *Die Rezeption Georg Büchners durch das deutsche Theater*. Berlin–Dahlem: Colloquium Verlag, 1957.

Viehweg, Wolfram. *Georg Büchners "Dantons Tod" auf dem deutschen Theater*. München: Laokoon-Verlag, 1964.

Viëtor, Karl. *Georg Büchner. Politik, Dichtung, Wissenschaft*. Bern: A. Franke Verlag, 1949.

Wiese, Benno von. "Georg Büchner. Die Tragödie des Nihilismus." *Die Deutsche Tragödie von Lessing bis Hebbel*. Hamburg: Hoffmann & Campe, 1961 ed., pp. 513–534.

IN ENGLISH

Baxandall, Lee. "Georg Büchner's *Danton's Death*." *Tulane Drama Review*, 6 (1961/62), No. 3, 136–149.

Benn, Maurice B. *The Drama of Revolt*. Cambridge, London, New York, Mebourne: Cambridge University Press, 1976.

Closs, August, "Nihilism and the Modern German Drama. Grabbe and Büchner." *Studies in German Literature*. London: Cresset Press, 1957, 147–163.

Cowen, Roy. "Identity and Conscience in Büchner's Works." *Germanic Review*, 43 (1968), 258–266.

Fischer, Heinz. "Some Marginal Notes on Georg Büchner." *Revue de littérature comparée*, 46 (1972), 255–258.

Fleissner, E. M. "Revolution as Theatre: *Danton's Death* and *Marat/Sade*." *Massachusetts Review*, 7 (1966), 548–556.

Hamburger, Michael. "Georg Büchner." *Evergreen Review* (1957), no. i, 68–98.

———. "Georg Büchner." *Reason and Energy*. London: Routledge & Paul, and New York: Grove Press, 1957.

Hauser, Ronald. *Georg Büchner*. New York: Twayne Publishers, 1974.

176 | BIBLIOGRAPHY

Jacobs, Margaret *"Dantons Tod"* and *"Woyzeck."* Ed. with introduction and notes, Manchester, 1954.

Kaufmann, Friedrich W. "Georg Büchner." *German Dramatists of the 19th Century.* Los Angeles: Lyman-house, 1940, 103–111.

Kayser, Wolfgang. " 'Grotesk! Grotesk!'—*Woyzeck*—The Romantic Comedy." *The Grotesque in Art and Literature*, transl. by Ulrich Weisstein. New York: Mc-Graw-Hill, 1966, 89–99.

Knight, Arthur H. J. "Some Considerations Relating to Georg Büchner's Opinions on History and the Drama and to his Play *Dantons Tod.*" *Modern Language Review*, 40 (1947), 70–81.

———. *Georg Büchner.* Oxford: Basil Blackwell, 1951.

Kresh, Joseph G. "Georg Büchner's Reputation as an Economic Radical." *Germanic Review*, 8 (1933), 44–51.

Lindenberger, Herbert S. *Georg Büchner.* Carbondale: Southern Illinois University Press, 1964.

Loram, Ian C. "Georg Kaiser's 'Der Soldat Tanaka': Vollendeter 'Woyzeck'?" *German Life and Letters*, 10 (1956–57), 43–48.

Maclean, H. "The Moral Conflict in Georg Büchner's *Dantons Tod.*" *Journal of the Australasian Modern Language Association*, 6 (May 1957), 25–33.

Majut, Rudolf. "Georg Büchner and Some English Thinkers." *Modern Language Review*, 48 (1953), 310–322.

———. "Some Literary Affiliations of Georg Büchner with England." *Modern Language Review*, 50 (1955), 30–48.

Murdoch, Brian. "Communication as a Dramatic Problem. Büchner, Chekhov, Hofmannsthal and Wesker." *Revue de littérature comparée*, 45 (1971), 40–56.

Parker, John J. "Some Reflections on Georg Büchner's *Lenz* and Its Principal Sources. The Oberlin Record." *German Life and Letters*, 21 (1967–68), 103–111.

Peacock, Ronald. "A Note on Georg Büchner's Plays." *German Life and Letters*, 10 (1955–57), 189–197.

Rosenberg, Ralph P. "Georg Büchner's Early Reception in America." *Journal of English and Germanic Philology*, 44 (1945), 270–273.

Schmidt, Henry J. *Satire, Caricature, and Perspectivism in the Works of Georg Büchner.* The Hague: Mouton, 1970.

Shaw, Leroy R. "Symbolism of Time in Georg Büchner's *Leonce and Lena.*" *Monatshefte für deutschen Unterricht,* 48 (1956), 221–230.

Steiner, George. *The Death of Tragedy.* New York: Hill & Wang, 1963, 270–281.

Stern, Joseph P. "A World of Suffering: Georg Büchner." *Re-Interpretations.* London: Thomas & Hudson, 1964, pp. 78–155.

Vickers, L. "Georg Büchner." *Nation,* 32 (1880), 224.

White, John S. "Georg Büchner or the Suffering Through the Father." *The American Imago,* 9 (1952), 365–427.

Yale/Theatre. Vol. 3, No. 3. *Special Büchner Issue.* Essays by Brustein, Gilman, John Simon, John Houseman, et al.

Zeidel, Edwin H. "A Note on Georg Büchner and Gerhart Hauptmann." *Journal of English and Germanic Philology,* 44 (1945), 87–88.

INDEX

Accomplices, The (*Die Mit-schuldigen*, Goethe), 145
Adamov, Arthur, 73, 163, 164, 165
Aeschylus, 165
Akademietheater (Vienna), 109
Alex, Liesel, 113
Anouilh, Jean, 110
Arbeiterzeitung (newspaper), 66
Arkadenhof (Vienna City Hall), 66
Arrabal, Fernando, 77
Arts Theatre (London), 149
Atkinson, Brooks, 68
Avant-garde, 111, 113, 165

Bach, Johann Sebastian, 162
Badische Neueste Nach-richten, 169
Bald Soprano, The (Ionesco), 165
Balser, Ewald, 70
Barbizon Plaza Theater (New York), 155
Barnes, Clive, 116, 156
Barnowsky, Viktor, 140, 141, 142
Baudelaire, Charles, 111
Bavarian State Theater, 145

Becker, August, 166
Beckett, Samuel, 112, 113, 116, 165
Beckmann, Heinz, 112, 113
Beethoven, Ludwig van, 117, 162
Belle-Alliance Theater (Berlin), 63
Benn, Maurice B., 172
Berg, Alban, 3, 157, 161–62, 164
Bergemann, Fritz, 3, 166
Berggren, Tommy, 149
Bergman, Ingmar, 147, 148
Bergmann, Alan, 77
Berliner Illustrierte Nachtaus-gabe, review quoted from, 69, 167
Berliner Tageblatt, 170
Bernau, Alfred, 65
Billington, Michael, 81, 115
Blacher, Boris, 164
Blau, Herbert, 76, 79
Bochumer Kammerspiele, 112
Bökenkampf, Werner von, 114
Borchardt, Peter, 157
Brahms, Hans, 109
Brahms, Johannes, 162
Brandauer, Klaus Maria, 119, 120
Brecht, Bertolt, 76, 111, 116, 138, 145, 152, 163–64

Brentano, Clemens, 105
Brion, Friederike, 39, 40
Brogle, Peter, 120, 150, 151
Broken Jug, The (Der zer-
    brochene Krug, Kleist),
    109
Brombacher, Peter, 117
Browne, R. L., 77
Bruck, Karl, 108
Brücke, Die (theatrical
    group), 154
Bruckner, Anton, 162
Büchner, Ernst Karl, 1, 7
Büchner, Georg
    biographical data, 1–3
    influence of, 161–65
    life and times of, 5–24
    political opinions of, 9–21
    view of art of, 25–31
Büchner, Ludwig, 3
Büchner, Wilhelm, 23, 31
Bulandra Theater (Buch-
    arest), 115
Burgtheater (Vienna), 70
Büttner, Ludwig, 129
Byron, George Gordon, Lord,
    58, 166

Caninenberg, Hans, 80
Caranitru, Ion, 116
Castro, Fidel, 76
Cato, Marcus, 26
Chaikin, Joseph, 156
Charles X (France), 20
Ciulei, Liviu, 116
Clarin, Hans, 150
Clarus, Johann Christian, 124–
    125, 157
Classic Stage Company
    (U.S.A.), 156
Commedia dell'arte, 90, 104,
    121
Compagnie du Centre Na-
    tional des arts (Ottawa),
    158

Daily Worker (newspaper),
    68–69, 167

Dallansky, Bruno, 110, 144
Danton's Death, 2, 3, 20, 22,
    25, 27, 30, 40, 104, 108,
    110, 139, 162, 165
    interpretation, 49–61
    productions, 61–86
    synopsis, 47–49
Danton's Death (von Einem's
    opera), 164
Darmstädter Echo (newspa-
    per), review quoted from,
    167
Davies, Michael, 111
Debussy, Claude, 117
Decarli, Bruno, 66
Degler, Marion, 110
Detmolder Landestheater, 167
Deutsche Allgemeine Zeitung,
    review quoted from, 167
Deutsches Schauspielhaus
    (Hamburg), 71, 85, 121,
    151
Deutches Theater (Berlin),
    64, 141
Deutsches Volkstheater
    (Vienna), 65
Deutsche Zeitung, 170
Domin, Friedrich, 68
Don Juan (Molière), 164
Dresdener Schauspielhaus, 66
Dumont, Eugen, 106
Dürrenmatt, Friedrich, 154
Düsseldorfer Bühne, 106
Düsseldorfer Schauspielhaus,
    70, 79
Dworsky, 141

Earth Spirit (Erdgeist, Wede-
    kind), 162
Edinburgh Festival, 115
Einem, Gottfried von, 164
Endgame (Beckett), 112
Endriss, Elisabeth, 155
Esterow, Milton, 76
Etlinger, Karl, 106, 108
Eugenia (student association),
    1, 8
existentialism, 70, 89

expressionism, 5, 64, 65, 136, 141, 143, 144, 161

Falckenberg, Otto, 65, 67
Falke, Walter, 71
Fantasio (de Musset), 105
Faust (Goethe), 133
Fechter, Paul, 67
Fehling, J., 143
Felber, Eugen, 143
Feuerbach, Ludwig, 129
Fielitz, Hans von, 65
Fifty Nine Theatre Company (England), 74, 111
Financial Times, The, review quoted from, 159, 171
Fischel, Herbert, 114
Flimm, Jürgen, 84, 85, 116, 117
Frankfurter Allgemeine Zeitung (newspaper), reviews from, excerpted, 79, 167, 168, 169, 171
Frankfurter Rundschau, 171
Frankfurter Schauspielhaus, 144
Frankfurter Zeitung, 170
Franklin, Richard, 145
Franz Joseph, Emperor, 109
Franzos, Karl Emil, 3, 170
Freie Volksbühne, Kurfürstendamm Theater (Berlin), 110, 144
French Revolution, 1, 13, 17, 20
Freud, Sigmund, 144

Gabel, Martin, 68
Gade, Svend, 140
Galloway, Myron, 160
German Democratic Republic (East Germany), 75
Gielen, Josef, 66, 167
Giliot, Michael, 111
Glasgow Citizens' Theatre, 81
Goethe, Johann Wolfgang von, 7, 27, 39, 57, 133, 145-46
Goldwater, Barry, Senator, 76

Grack, Günter, 85
Grand Magic Circus (Paris), 121
Graumann, Max, 63
Grillon, 112
Gründgens, Gustaf, 65, 69, 71
Gussow, Mel, 152
Gutzkow, Karl, 3, 16, 22, 23

Haas, Tom, 152
Haas, Willy, 76
Hack, Keith, 81
Halbe, Max, 105
Hamburger Anzeiger, 168
Hamburger Fremdenblatt (newspaper), review quoted from, 107, 168
Hamburger Kammerspiele, 65, 108
Hamlet (Shakespeare), 97, 146, 168
Hannele (*Hanneles Himmelfahrt*, Hauptmann), 161
Hannoversche Schauspielhaus, das (Hannover), 157
Hartmann, Paul, 67
Hasenclever, Walter, 162
Hauptmann, Gerhart, 161
Hauser, Ronald, 165
Heartfield, 141
Heine, Heinrich, 96
Henninger, Rolf, 113
Henschel the Carter (*Fuhrmann Henschel*, Hauptmann), 161
Hensel, Georg, 71, 79, 158
Herbiet, Jean, 158
Herder, Johann Gottfried, 26, 27, 166
Hessian Messenger, The, 2, 14-21, 45, 93, 94, 104, 109
Hessisches Landestheater (Darmstadt), 70, 71
Hilpert, Heinz, 109, 110
Hinkemann (Toller), 162
Hörbiger, Christiane, 154
Houseman, John, 68
Howard, Dennis, 116

Hugo, Victor, 2, 23
Humanity (Die Menschen, Hasenclever), 162

Ignée, Wolfgang, 171
Ihering, Herbert, 107
Ionesco, Eugène, 116, 165
Irving, Jules, 76, 79
Ivernel, Daniel, 73

Jacobi, Johannes, 171
Jacobs, Margaret, 126
Jacobson, Siegfried, 142
Jaegle, Pastor Johann Jakob, 1, 8
Jaegle, Louise Wilhelmine, 1, 8
John, Gottfried, 79
Johnson, Lyndon Baines, President, 76
Jones, J. C., 116
Jungbauer, Hans, 144

Kafka, Franz, 36, 78
Kaiser, Joachim, 169
Kalow, Gert, 79, 169
Katakombe, Die (Frankfurt), 113
Kauffmann, Stanley, 146
Kautek, Rudolf, 114
Kay, Charles, 80
Kelling, Gerhard, 157
Kerr, Alfred, 108, 143
Kilian, Eugen, 63, 139
Kirchner, Alfred, 157
Kleber, Hans, 117
Kleiber, Erich, 163
Klein, Cäsar, 141
Klein, Paul, 108
Kleist, Heinrich von, 109, 165
Klonck, Erhardt, 72
Klöpfer, Eugen, 141, 142
Knuth, Gustav, 69
Kölner Schauspielhaus (Cologne), 144
König, Otto, 142
Kotthaus, Eva, 150
Krapp, Helmut, 135, 136
Kraus, Fritz, 144

Krone Circus, 120, 121
Krottendorf, Ida, 144
Krushchev, Nikita, 75
Kuba (nom de plume), 75
Kuhl, J. K., 2, 22
Kuhlmann, Harold, 84

La Mama—Plexus II (English theatrical company), 149, 151, 152
Lang, Harold, 74
Lasse, Friedrich, 65
Lautréamont, Isidore Ducasse, le comte de, 78
Leber, Hugo, 154
Lehmann, Werner, 3, 152, 166
Lehmann-Brauns, Elke, 83
Lenz, 2, 3, 30, 117
  interpretation, 34–46
  synopsis, 31–34
Lenz, Jakob Michael, 2, 31
Leonce and Lena, 2, 3, 23, 25, 27, 30, 40, 61, 140, 144, 150, 159, 165
  interpretation, 89–104
  productions, 104–121
  synopsis, 87–89
Lessingtheater (Berlin), 107, 141
Lewis, Jeff, 160
Lichtenhahn, Fritz, 151
Lietzau, Hans, 145, 146
Lincoln Center Repertory Theater (New York), 76
Lindemann, Gustav, 106
Lippisches Landestheater (Detmold), 72
Lorre, Peter, 67
Louis Philippe, King, 20
Lück, Heinz Gerhard, 84
Lucretia Borgia (Hugo, translated by Büchner), 2, 23
Ludwig I, Grand Duke of Hesse, 6
Ludwig II, Grand Duke of Hesse, 6
Ludwigsburg Summer Festival, 111, 112
Lukács, Georg, 128, 129

Lützenkirchen, Mathieu, 63
Lyric Theatre (Hammer-
  smith), 74

Man is Man (Mann ist Mann,
  Brecht), 164
Manas, Sylvia, 120
Mannheimer Generalanzeiger
  (newspaper), 108, 143
Mao-Tse-tung, 76
Marbacher Zeitung, 168
Marburger Schauspiel, 72
Maria Tudor (Hugo, trans-
  lated by Büchner), 2, 23
Marowitz, Charles, 155
Martens, Wolfgang, 133
Martin, Christoph, 156
Martin, Karl Heinz, 67
Marx, Karl, 11, 14, 129, 143
Mautner, Franz, 132, 136, 137,
  170
Mayer, Hans, 128
McDianmid, Ian, 81
McGoohan, Patrick, 74
Mehring, Wolfram, 112
"Mémoire sur le système ner-
  veux du barbeau", 2, 23
Mensching, Herbert, 85
Mentwich, Marianne, 119
Mercury Theatre, 68, 69
Meschke, Michael, 82, 83
Metternich, Klemens Wenzel,
  Prince, 5
Michaelis, Rolf, 85
Mielziner, Jo, 77
Miller, Jonathan, 80
Minks, Wilfried, 80, 118
Mirbt, Felix, 158
Molière, Jean-Baptiste Po-
  quelin, 99, 164
Montreal Star, The (newspa-
  per), review quoted from,
  171
Mörike, Eduard, 78
Mues, Dietmar, 84
Mülher, Robert, 169
Münchener Kammerspiele
  (Munich), 65, 67, 71

Münchener Post (newspaper),
  review quoted from, 139,
  170
Münchener Puppentheater
  (Munich Puppet The-
  ater), 113
Musset, Alfred, 105
Müthel, Lothar, 108

Napoleon Bonaparte, 6, 7, 20,
  96
National Socialism (Nazi Germany), 69, 109–110, 144,
  164
Nationaltheater (Mannheim),
  116, 117, 143
National Theatre (London),
  80
National-Zeitung (newspa-
  per), review quoted from,
  154, 171
naturalism, 5, 30, 61, 128, 135,
  136, 149, 152, 161
Neher, Caspar, 110, 144, 164
Nel, Christof, 157
Neue Freie Presse (newspaper), 106, 168
Neuenfels, Hans, 77, 78
Neues Wiener Journal (newspaper), reviews from, excerpted, 106, 143
Neues Wiener Tagblatt
  (newspaper), 141
New York Times, reviews
  from, excerpted, 77, 116,
  156, 167, 168, 171
Nielson, Monica, 82

Oberlin, Jean-Frédéric, 30, 31
Österreichische Volkszeitung
  (newspaper), review
  quoted from, 141
Open Space (London the-
  ater), 155
Oppel, Horst, 138
Orff, Carl, 108
Orth, Elisabeth, 146
Ostendorf, Jens Peter, 117

Ottawa Citizen, The (newspaper), review quoted from, 171

Palitzsch, Peter, 158
Pandora's Box (*Die Büchse der Pandora*, Wedekind), 162
Parody, The (Adamov), 165
Persecution and Assassination of Marat as Performed by the Inmates of the Asylum of Charenton under the Direction of the Marquis de Sade, The (Weiss), 165
Pietro Aretino, 24
Piscator, Erwin, 72
Pistoni, Roberto, 153
Planchon, Roger, 116
Plummer, Christopher, 80
Polish Stary Teatr (Cracow), 146
Ponce de Leon (Brentano), 105
Presse, Die (newspaper), review quoted from, 118, 169
Propst, Herbert, 114
Proust, Marcel, 78
Prowse, Philip, 81
Puecher, Virginio, 152, 153, 157

Rappard, Gillis van, 71
Raynor, Henry, 149, 151
Regnier, Charles, 144
Rehberg, Hans-Michel, 84, 85
Reichmann, Wolfgang, 80
Reinbacher, Wolfgang, 80
Reinhardt, Max, 3, 64, 65, 66, 68, 85, 141, 142
Residenzbühne (Vienna), 140
Residenztheater (Munich), 63, 139
Residenztheater (Vienna), 106, 121
Reuss, Eduard, 8
Rheinischer Merkur, reviews quoted from, 168, 171

Rismondo, Piero, 118
Robertson, Patrick, 80
Roesner, Winfried, 116
Rohde, Willi, 70
Rolant, Albert, 114
Roller, Alfred, 139
romanticism, 10, 96, 97, 101, 105
Rose, Jürgen, 146
Ross, Colin, 139
Rott, Adolf, 70
Rousseau, Jean-Jacques, 16, 42
Royal Academy of Dramatic Art, 145
Royal Court Theatre (England), 111
Royal Dramatic Theater (Stockholm), 147
Rudolf, Niels-Peter, 151
Ruhr Festival (Recklinghausen), 150
Rundt, Arthur, 140

Sadler's Wells, 110, 144
Saint-Simon movement, 8, 9
Salzburger Summer Festival, 118, 119, 164
Sartre, Jean Paul, 70
Savary, Jerome, 121
Schaaf, Johannes, 118, 119, 120
Schalla, Hans, 70, 75, 76, 112, 113
Schell, Maximilian, 110
Scherreiks, Herbert, 112
Schiff, Else, 63
Schiller, Friedrich von, 7, 27
Schillertheater (Berlin), 72, 143
Schindler, Hans, 107
Schmidt, Willi, 150, 151
Schoenberg, Arnold, 162
Schofield, David, 156
Schreiber, Helene, 147
Schuh, Oscar Fritz, 144, 145
Schumann, Robert, 117
Schwab-Felisch, Hans, 80, 151
Schwäbische Zeitung (newspaper), 169

Schweikart, Hans, 71
Seidel, Annemarie, 108
Sellner, Gustav Rudolf, 71
Shakespeare, William, 7, 27, 56, 90, 104, 155, 164
Shaliko Company, 156
Smetana, Bedřich, 117
Sokoloff, Wladimir, 68
Sophocles, 165
Speiser, Kitty, 115
Spring's Awakening (Frühlingserwachen, Wedekind), 162
Staatliches Schauspielhaus (Berlin), 69, 108
Staatstheater (Stuttgart), 157
Städtische Bühnen (Bochum), 70
Stadttheater (Giessen), 72
Stalin, Joseph, 75, 76
Stanchina, Peter, 144
Steiger, Edgar, 167
Steinrück, Albert, 140, 141
Stern, J. P., 127
storm and stress (Sturm und Drang) movement, 25, 26, 27, 31, 96
Strindberg, August, 112
Stroux, Karl-Heinz, 80
Strudthoff, Ingeborg, 167, 168, 170
Sturm, Eduard, 106
Stuttgarter Nachrichten (newspaper), reviews quoted from, 167, 168
Stuttgarter Zeitung (newspaper), reviews quoted from, 167, 171
Süddeutsche Zeitung (newspaper), review quoted from, 167, 168, 169
surrealism, 111, 157, 163
Suschka, Herbert, 76
Swinarski, 146, 147
Symond, Robert, 76

Tag, Der (newspaper), review from, 63, 166

Tagesspiegel, Der (newspaper), review quoted from, 168
Tartuffe, 99
Teatro Stabile (Turin), 130, 152, 153
theater of the absurd, 5, 61, 104, 112, 164
Théâtre Franco-Allemand (Paris), 111
Théâtre National Populaire, 73
Thil, Baron du Bos du, 6
Times The (London), reviews from, excerpted, 74, 77, 110, 111, 115, 144, 145, 149, 167, 168, 170, 171
Toller, Ernst, 62
Trofarelli, Isa Falleni, 130
Trotzki in Exil (Weiss), 165

Verwoerd, Henrik F., 76
Viehweg, Wolfram, 167
Viëtor, Karl, 125, 129, 133, 134, 139, 170
Vilar, Jean, 73, 74
Vivian Beaumont Theater (Lincoln Center for the Performing Arts), 76, 77
Völker, Klaus, 152
Völkischer Beobachter, 168
Volksbühne (Berlin), 67, 109
Volkstheater (Vienna), 114

Waiting for Godot (Beckett), 165
Wallis, Bill, 111
Walser, Karl, 107
Wälterlin, Oskar, 71
Wardle, Irving, 81
Weavers, The (Die Weber, Hauptmann), 161
Wedekind, Frank, 162
Weichert, Richard, 107
Weidig, Friedrich, Ludwig, 1, 2, 14, 15, 16, 20, 22
Weiler, A. H., 155
Weiss, Peter, 165
Welles, Orson, 68, 69

Welt, Die (newspaper), reviews from, excerpted, 72, 76, 167, 169
Werth, Wolfgang, 145
Werther, Otto, 65
Wetkens, Wolf, 159
Wiener Abendpost (newspaper), 141
Wiener Arbeiterzeitung (newspaper), reviews quoted from, 106, 142, 170
Wiese, Benno von, 126
Wilbrand, Prof., 134
Wild, Winfried, 112, 120
Wildschild, Herta, 108
Wolf, Ludwig, 106
Wolff, Karl, 63
Wolzogen, Ernst von, 105
Woostin, Frau, 125
Woyzeck, 3, 11, 23, 24, 27, 30, 63, 89, 92, 93, 95, 104, 107, 114, 121, 161-63
    interpretation, 124-37
    the *Woyzeck* problem, 137-39
    productions, 139-60
    synopsis, 122-24
Woyzeck, Wolfgang Johann Christian, 30, 124
Wozzeck (Berg's opera), 3, 157, 162-63, 164, 170
Wright, Max, 116
Wymark, Patrick, 74

Yale School of Drama Repertory Theater, 152
Young Germany movement, 22

Zampa, Giorgio, 152
Zechell, Josef, 68
Zehder, H., 72
Zeit, Die (newspaper), reviews quoted from, 85, 168, 171
Ziermann, Horst, 121
Zuckmayer, Carl, 161
Züricher Schauspielhaus, 71, 154